PHILOSOPHY OF HINDUISM

PHILOSOPHY OF HINDUISM

DR. B. R. AMBEDKAR

ISBN: 978-93-5614-802-4

Published: -

LECTOR HOUSE

LECTOR HOUSE LLP
E-MAIL: info@lectorhouse.com

PHILOSOPHY OF HINDUISM

BY

DR. B. R. AMBEDKAR

PHILOSOPHY OF HINDUISM

I.

What is the philosophy of Hinduism? This is a question which arises in its logical sequence. But apart from its logical sequence its importance is such that it can never be omitted from consideration. Without it no one can understand the aims and ideals of Hinduism.

It is obvious that such a study must be preceded by a certain amount of what may be called clearing of the ground and defining of the terms involved.

At the outset it may be asked what does this proposed title comprehend? Is this title of the Philosophy of Hinduism of the same nature as that of the Philosophy of Religion? I wish I could commit myself one way or the other on this point. Indeed I cannot. I have read a good deal on the subject, but I confess I have not got a clear idea of what is meant by Philosophy of Religion. This is probably due to two facts. In the first place while religion is something definite, there is nothing definite[1] as to what is to be included in the term philosophy. In the second place Philosophy and Religion have been adversaries if not actual antagonists as may be seen from the story of the philosopher and the theologian. According to the story, the two were engaged in disputation and the theologian accused the philosopher that he was "like a blind man in a dark room, looking for a black cat which was not there." In reply the philosopher charged the theologian saying that "he was like a blind man in the dark room, looking for a black cat which was not there but he declared to have found there." Perhaps it is the unhappy choice of the title — Philosophy of Religion—which is responsible for causing confusion in the matter of the exact definition of its field. The nearest approach to an intelligible statement as to the exact subject matter of Philosophy of Religion I find in Prof. Pringle-Pattison who observes[2]:—

> "A few words may be useful at the outset as an indication of what we commonly mean by the Philosophy of Religion. Plato described philosophy long ago as the synoptic view of things. That is to say, it is the attempt to see things together-to keep all the main features of the world in view, and to grasp them in their relation to one another as parts of one whole. Only thus can we acquire a sense of proportion and estimate aright the significance of any particular range of facts for our ultimate conclusions about

[1] See Article on `Philosophy' in Munro's Encyclopaedia of Education.

[2] The Philosophy of Religion. Oxf. pages 1-2.

the nature of the world-process and the world-ground. Accordingly, the philosophy of any particular department of experience, the Philosophy of Religion, the Philosophy of Art, the Philosophy of Law, is to be taken as meaning an analysis and interpretation of the experience in question in its bearing upon our view of man and the world in which he lives. And when the facts upon which we concentrate are so universal, and in their nature so remarkable, as those disclosed by the history of religion—the philosophy of man's religious experience—cannot but exercise a determining influence upon our general philosophical conclusions. In fact with many writers the particular discussion tends to merge in the more general."

"The facts with which a philosophy of religion has to deal are supplied by the history of religion, in the most comprehensive sense of that term. As Tiele puts it, "all religions of the civilized and uncivilized world, dead and living," is a `historical and psychological phenomenon' in all its manifestations. These facts, it should be noted, constitute the data of the philosophy of religion; they do not themselves constitute a `philosophy' or, in Tiele's use of the term, a `science' of religion. `If,' he says, 'I have minutely described all the religions in existence, their doctrines, myths and customs, the observances they inculcate, and the organization of their adherents, tracing the different religions from their origin to their bloom and decay, I have merely collected the materials with which the science of religion works.' 'The historical record, however complete, is not enough; pure history is not philosophy. To achieve a philosophy of religion we should be able to discover in the varied manifestations a common principle to whose roots in human nature we can point, whose evolution we can trace by intelligible-stages from lower to higher and more adequate forms, as well as its intimate relations with the other main factors in human civilization.'"

If this is Philosophy of Religion it appears to me that it is merely a different name for that department of study, which is called comparative religion with the added aim of discovering a common principle in the varied manifestations of religion. Whatever be the scope and value of such a study, I am using the title Philosophy of Religion to denote something quite different from the sense and aim given to it by Prof. Pringle-Pattison. I am using the word Philosophy in its original sense, which was two-fold. It meant teachings as it did when people spoke of the philosophy of Socrates or the philosophy of Plato. In another sense it meant critical reason used in passing judgements upon things and events. Proceeding on this basis Philosophy of Religion is to me not a merely descriptive science. I regard it as being both descriptive as well as normative. In so far as it deals with the teachings of a Religion, Philosophy of Religion becomes a descriptive science. In so far as it involves the use of critical reason for passing judgement on those teachings, the Philosophy of Religion becomes a normative science. From this it will be clear what I shall be concerned with in this study of the Philosophy of Hinduism. To be explicit I shall be putting Hinduism on its trial to assess its worth as a way of life.

Here is one part of the ground cleared. There remains another part to be cleared. That concerns the ascertainment of the factors concerned and the definitions of the terms I shall be using.

A study of the Philosophy of Religion it seems to me involves the determination of three dimensions. I call them dimensions because they are like the unknown quantities contained as factors in a product. One must ascertain and define these dimensions of the Philosophy of Religion if an examination of it is to be fruitful.

Of the three dimensions, Religion is the first. One must therefore define what he understands by religion in order to avoid argument being directed at cross-purposes. This is particularly necessary in the case of Religion for the reason that there is no agreement as to its exact definition. This is no place to enter upon an elaborate consideration of this question. I will therefore content myself by stating the meaning in which I am using the word in the discussion, which follows.

I am using the word Religion to mean Theology. This will perhaps be insufficient for the purposes of definition. For there are different kinds of Theologies and I must particularize which one I mean. Historically there have been two Theologies spoken of from ancient times. *Mythical* theology and *Civil* theology. The Greeks who distinguished them gave each a definite content. By Mythical theology they meant the tales of gods and their doings told in or implied by current imaginative literature. Civil theology according to them consisted of the knowledge of the various feasts and fasts of the State Calendar and the ritual appropriate to them. I am not using the word theology in either of these two senses of that word. I mean by theology *natural theology*[3] which is the doctrine of God and the divine, as an integral part of the theory of nature. As traditionally understood there are three thesis which `natural theology' propounds. (1) That God exists and is the author of what we call nature or universe (2) That God controls all the events which make nature and (3) God exercises a government over mankind in accordance with his sovereign moral law.

I am aware there is another class of theology known as *Revealed Theology*—spontaneous self disclosure of divine reality—which may be distinguished from *Natural theology*. But this distinction does not really matter. For as has been pointed out[4] that a revelation may either "leave the results won by *Natural theology* standing without modifications, merely supplementing them by further knowledge not attainable by unassisted human effort" or it "may transform Natural theology in such a way that all the truths of natural theology would acquire richer and deeper meaning when seen in the light of a true revelation." But the view that a genuine *natural theology* and a genuine *revelation theology* might stand in real contradiction may be safely excluded as not being possible.

---

[3] Natural Theology as a distinct department of study owes its origin to Plato-see Laws.

[4] A. E. Taylor. "The Faith of a Moralist", p. 19.

Taking the three thesis of Theology namely (1) the existence of God, (2) God's providential government of the universe and (3) God's moral government of mankind, I take Religion to mean the propounding of an ideal scheme of divine governance the aim and object of which is to make the social order in which men live a moral order. This is what I understand by Religion and this is the sense in which I shall be using the term Religion in this discussion.

The second dimension is to know the ideal scheme for which a Religion stands. To define what is the fixed, permanent and dominant part in the religion of any society and to separate its essential characteristics from those which are unessential is often very difficult. The reason for this difficulty in all probability lies in the difficulty pointed out by Prof. Robertson Smith[5] when he says:—

> "The traditional usage of religion had grown up gradually in the course of many centuries, and reflected habits of thought, characteristic of very diverse stages of man's intellectual and moral development. No conception of the nature of the gods could possibly afford the clue to all parts of that motley complex of rites and ceremonies which the later paganism had received by inheritance, from a series of ancestors in every state of culture from pure savagery upwards. The record of the religious thought of mankind, as it is embodied in religious institutions, resembles the geological record of the history of the earth's crust; the new and the old are preserved side by side, or rather layer upon layer."

The same thing has happened in India. Speaking about the growth of Religion in India, says Prof. Max Muller:—

> "We have seen a religion growing up from stage to stage, from the simplest childish prayers to the highest metaphysical abstractions. In the majority of the hymns of the Veda we might recognise the childhood; in the Brahmanas and their sacrificial, domestic and moral ordinances the busy manhood; in the Upanishads the old age of the Vedic religion. We could have well understood if, with the historical progress of the Indian mind, they had discarded the purely childish prayers as soon as they had arrived at the maturity of the Brahamans; and if, when the vanity of sacrifices and the real character of the old gods had once been recognised, they would have been superseded by the more exalted religion of the Upanishads. But it was not so. Every religious thought that had once found expression in India, that had once been handed down as a sacred heirloom, was preserved, and the thoughts of the three historical periods, the childhood, the manhood, and the old age of the Indian nation, were made to do permanent service in the three stages of the life of every individual. Thus alone can we explain how the same sacred code, the Veda, contains not only the records of different phases of religious thought, but of doctrines which we may call almost diametrically opposed to each

[5] The Religion of the Semites (1927).

other."

But this difficulty is not so great in the case of Religions which are *positive* religions. The fundamental characteristic of *positive* Religions, is that they have not grown up like primitive religions, under the action of unconscious forces operating silently from age to age, but trace their origin to the teaching of great religious innovators, who spoke as the organs of a divine revelation. Being the result of conscious formulations the philosophy of a religion which is positive is easy to find and easy to state. Hinduism like Judaism, Christianity and Islam is in the main a positive religion. One does not have to search for its scheme of divine governance. It is not like an unwritten constitution. On the Hindu scheme of divine governance is enshrined in a written constitution and any one who cares to know it will find it laid bare in that Sacred Book called the Manu Smriti, a divine Code which lays down the rules which govern the religious, ritualistic and social life of the Hindus in minute detail and which must be regarded as the Bible of the Hindus and containing the philosophy of Hinduism.

The third dimension in the philosophy of religion is the criterion[6] to be adopted for judging the value of the ideal scheme of divine governance for which a given Religion stands. Religion must be put on its trial. By what criterion shall it be judged? That leads to the definition of the norm. Of the three dimensions this third one is the most difficult one to be ascertained and defined.

Unfortunately the question does not appear to have been tackled although much has been written on the philosophy of Religion and certainly no method has been found for satisfactorily dealing with the problem. One is left to one's own method for determining the issue. As for myself I think it is safe to proceed on the view that to know the philosophy of any movement or any institution one must study the revolutions which the movement or the institution has undergone. Revolution is the mother of philosophy and if it is not the mother of philosophy it is a lamp which illuminates philosophy. Religion is no exception to this rule. To me therefore it seems quite evident that the best method to ascertain the criterion by which to judge the philosophy of Religion is to study the Revolutions which religion has undergone. That is the method which I propose to adopt.

Students of History are familiar with one Religious Revolution. That Revolution was concerned with the sphere of Religion and the extent of its authority. There was a time when Religion had covered the whole field of human knowledge and claimed infallibility for what it taught. It covered astronomy and taught a theory of the universe according to which the earth is at rest in the center of the universe, while the sun, moon, planets and system of fixed stars revolve round it

[6] Some students of the Philosophy of Religion seem to regard the study of the first two dimensions as all that the field of Philosophy of religion need include. They do not seem to recognize that a consideration of the third dimension is necessary part of the study of the Philosophy of Religion. As an illustration of this see the Article on Theology by Mr. D. S. Adamas in 'Hastings Encyclopedia of Religion and Ethics', Volume XII, page 393. I dissent from this view. The difference is probably due to the fact that I regard Philosophy of Religion as a normative study and as a descriptive study. I do not think that there can be such a thing as a general Philosophy of Religion. I believe each Religion has its particular philosophy. To me there is no Philosophy of Religion. There is a philosophy of a Religion.

each in its own sphere. It included biology and geology and propounded the view that the growth of life on the earth had been created all at once and had contained from the time of creation onwards, all the heavenly bodies that it now contains and all kinds of animals of plants. It claimed medicine to be its province and taught that disease was either a divine visitation as punishment for sin or it was the work of demons and that it could be cured by the intervention of saints, either in person or through their holy relics; or by prayers or pilgrimages; or (when due to demons) by exorcism and by treatment which the demons (and the patient) found disgusting. It also claimed physiology and psychology to be its domain and taught that the body and soul were two distinct substances.

Bit by bit this vast Empire of Religion was destroyed. The Copernican Revolution freed astronomy from the domination of Religion. The Darwinian Revolution freed biology and geology from the trammels of Religion. The authority of theology in medicine is not yet completely destroyed. Its intervention in medical questions still continues. Opinion on such subjects as birth-control, abortion and sterilization of the defective are still influenced by theological dogmas. Psychology has not completely freed itself from its entanglements. None the less Darwinism was such a severe blow that the authority of theology was shattered all over to such an extent that it never afterwards made any serious effort to remain its lost empire.

It is quite natural that this disruption of the Empire of Religion should be treated as a great Revolution. It is the result of the warfare which science waged against theology for 400 years, in which many pitched battles were fought between the two and the excitement caused by them was so great that nobody could fail to be impressed by the revolution that was blazing on.

There is no doubt that this religious revolution has been a great blessing. It has established freedom of thought. It has enabled society "to assume control of itself, making its own the world it once shared with superstition, facing undaunted the things of its former fears, and so carving out for itself, from the realm of mystery in which it lies, a sphere of unhampered action and a field of independent thought." The process of secularisation is not only welcomed by scientists for making civilization—as distinguished from culture—possible, even Religious men and women have come to feel that much of what theology taught was unnecessary and a mere hindrance to the religious life and that this chopping of its wild growth was a welcome process.

But for ascertaining the norm for judging the philosophy of Religion we must turn to another and a different kind of Revolution which Religion has undergone. That Revolution touches the nature and content of ruling conceptions of the relations of God to man, of Society to man and of man to man. How great was this revolution can be seen from the differences which divide savage society from civilized society.

Strange as it may seem no systematic study of this Religious Revolution has so far been made. None the less this Revolution is so great and so immense that it has brought about a complete transformation in the nature of Religion as it is taken to be by savage society and by civilized society although very few seem to be aware of it.

To begin with the comparison between savage society and civilized society.

In the religion of the savage one is struck by the presence of two things. First is the performance of rites and ceremonies, the practice of magic or tabu and the worship of fetish or totem. The second thing that is noticeable is that the rites, ceremonies, magic, tabu, totem and fetish are conspicuous by their connection with certain occasions. These occasions are chiefly those, which represent the crises of human life. The events such as birth, the birth of the first born, attaining manhood, reaching puberty, marriage, sickness, death and war are the usual occasions which are marked out for the performance of rites and ceremonies, the use of magic and the worship of the totem.

Students of the origin and history of Religion have sought to explain the origin and substance of religion by reference to either magic, tabu and totem and the rites and ceremonies connected therewith, and have deemed the occasions with which they are connected as of no account. Consequently we have theories explaining religion as having arisen in magic or as having arisen in *fetishism*. Nothing can be a greater error than this. It is true that savage society practices magic, believes in tabu and worships the totem. But it is wrong to suppose that these constitute the religion or form the source of religion. To take such a view is to elevate what is incidental to the position of the principal.

The principal thing in the Religion of the savage are the elemental facts of human existence such as life, death, birth, marriage etc. Magic, tabu, totem are things which are incidental. Magic, tabu, totem, fetish etc., are not the ends. They are only the means. The end is life and the preservation of life. Magic, tabu etc., are resorted to by the savage society not for their own sake but to conserve life and to *exercise* evil influences from doing harm to life. Thus understood the religion of the savage society was concerned with life and the preservation of life and it is these life processes which constitute the substance and source of the religion of the savage society. So great was the concern of the savage society for life and the preservation of life that it made them the basis of its religion. So central were the life processes in the religion of the savage society that everything, which affected them, became part of its religion. The ceremonies of the savage society were not only concerned with the events of birth, attaining of manhood, puberty, marriage, sickness, death and war they were also concerned with food. Among pastoral peoples the flocks and herds are sacred. Among agricultural peoples seedtime and harvest are marked by ceremonials performed with some reference to the growth and the preservation of the crops. Likewise drought, pestilence, and other strange, irregular phenomena of nature occasion the performance of ceremonials. Why should such occasions as harvest and famine be accompanied by religious ceremonies? Why is magic, tabu, totem be of such importance to the savage. The only answer is that they all affect the preservation of life. The process of life and its preservation form the main purpose. Life and preservation of life is the core and centre of the Religion of the savage society. As pointed out by Prof. Crawley the religion of the savage begins and ends with the affirmation and conservation of life.

In life and preservation of life consists the religion of the savage. What is however true of the religion of the savage is true of all religions wherever they are found for the simple reason that constitutes the essence of religion. It is true that in the present day society with its theological refinements this essence of religion has become hidden from view and is even forgotten. But that life and the preservation of life constitute the essence of religion even in the present day society is beyond question. This is well illustrated by Prof. Crowley. When speaking of the religious life of man in the present day society, he says how—

> "a man's religion does not enter into his professional or social hours, his scientific or artistic moments; practically its chief claims are settled on one day in the week from which ordinary worldly concerns are excluded. In fact, his life is in two parts; but the moiety with which religion is concerned is the elemental. Serious thinking on ultimate questions of life and death is, roughly speaking, the essence of his Sabbath; add to this the habit of prayer, giving the thanks at meals, and the subconscious feeling that birth and death, continuation and marriage are rightly solemnized by religion, while business and pleasure may possibly be consecrated, but only metaphorically or by an overflow of religious feeling."

Comparing this description of the religious concerns of the man in the present day society with that of the savage, who can deny that the religion is essentially the same, both in theory and practice whether one speaks of the religion of the savage society or of the civilized society.

It is therefore clear that savage and civilized societies agree in one respect. In both the central interests of religion—namely in the life processes by which individuals are preserved and the race maintained—are the same. In this there is no real difference between the two. But they differ in two other important respects.

In the first place in the religion of the savage society there is no trace of the idea of God. In the second place in the religion of the savage society there is no bond between morality and Religion. In the savage society there is religion without God. In the savage society there is morality but it is independent of Religion.

How and when the idea of God became fused in Religion it is not possible to say. It may be that the idea of God had its origin in the worship of the Great Man in Society, the Hero—giving rise to theism—with its faith in its living God. It may be that the idea of God came into existence as a result of the purely philosophical speculation upon the problem as to who created life—giving rise to Deism—with its belief in God as Architect of the Universe.[7] In any case the idea of God is not integral to Religion. How it got fused into Religion it is difficult to explain. With regard to the relation between Religion and Morality this much may be safely said. Though the relation between God and Religion is not quite integral, the relation between Religion and morality is. Both religion and morality are connected with the same elemental facts of human existence—namely life, death, birth and mar-

[7] That the idea of God has evolved from both these directions is well illustrated by Hinduism. Compare the idea of Indra as God and the idea of Bramha as God.

riage. Religion consecrates these life processes while morality furnishes rules for their preservation. Religion in consecrating the elemental facts and processes of life came to consecrate also the rules laid down by Society for their preservation. Looked at from this point it is easily explained why the bond between Religion and Morality took place. It was more intimate and more natural than the bond between Religion and God. But when exactly this fusion between Religion and Morality took place it is not easy to say.

Be that as it may, the fact remains that the religion of the Civilized Society differs from that of the Savage Society into two important features. In civilized society God comes in the scheme of Religion. In civilized society morality becomes sanctified by Religion.

This is the first stage in the Religious Revolution I am speaking of. This Religious Revolution must not be supposed to have been ended here with the emergence of these two new features in the development of religion. The two ideas having become part of the constitution of the Religion of the Civilized Society have undergone further changes which have revolutionized their meaning and their moral significance. The second stage of the Religious Revolution marks a very radical change. The contrast is so big that civilized society has become split into two, antique society and modern society, so that instead of speaking of the religion of the civilized society it becomes necessary to speak of the religion of antique society as against the religion of modern society.

The religious revolution, which marks off antique society from modern society, is far greater than the religious revolution, which divides savage society from civilized society. Its dimensions will be obvious from the differences it has brought about in the conceptions regarding the relations between God, Society and Man.

The first point of difference relates to the composition of society.

Every human being, without choice on his own part, but simply in virtue of his birth and upbringing, becomes a member of what we call a *natural* society. He belongs that is to a certain family and a certain nation. This membership lays upon him definite obligations and duties which he is called upon to fulfil as a matter of course and on pain of social penalties and disabilities while at the same time it confers upon him certain social rights and advantages. In this respect the ancient and modern worlds are alike. But in the words of Prof. Smith[8]:—

> "There is this important difference, that the tribal or national societies of the ancient world were not strictly natural in the modern sense of the word, for the gods had their part and place in them equally with men. The circle into which a man was born was not simply a group of kinsfolk and fellow citizens, but embraced also certain divine beings, the gods of the family and of the state, which to the ancient mind were as much a part of the particular community with which they stood connected as the human members of the social circle. The relation between the gods of antiquity and their worshippers was expressed in the language of human

[8] Smith *Ibid*.

relationship, and this language was not taken in a figurative sense but with strict literally. If a god was spoken of as father and his worshippers as his offspring, the meaning was that the worshippers were literally of his stock, that he and they made up one natural family with reciprocal family duties to one another. Or, again, if the god was addressed as king, and worshippers called themselves his servants, they meant that the supreme guidance of the state was actually in his hands, and accordingly the organisation of the state included provision for consulting his will and obtaining his direction in all weighty matters, also provision for approaching him as king with due homage and tribute."

"Thus a man was born into a fixed relation to certain gods as surely as he was born into relation to his fellow men; and his religion, that is, the part of conduct which was determined by his relation to the gods, was simply one side of the general scheme of conduct prescribed for him by his position as a member of society. There was no separation between the spheres of religion and of ordinary life. Every social act had a reference to the gods as well as to men, for the social body was not made up of men only, but of gods and men."

Thus in ancient Society men and their Gods formed a social and political as well as a religious whole. Religion was founded on kinship between the God and his worshippers. Modern Society has eliminated God from its composition. It consists of men only.

The second point of difference between antique and modern society relates to the bond between God and Society. In the antique world the various communities

"believed in the existence of many Gods, for they accepted as real the Gods of their enemies as well as their own, but they did not worship the strange Gods from whom they had no favour to expect, and on whom their gifts and offerings would have been thrown away.... Each group had its own God, or perhaps a God and Goddess, to whom the other Gods bore no relation whatever."[9]

The God of the antique society was an exclusive God. God was owned by and bound to one singly community. This is largely to be accounted for by

"the share taken by the Gods in the feuds and wars of their worshippers. The enemies of the God and the enemies of his people are identical; even in the Old Testament `the enemies of Jehovah' are originally nothing else than the enemies of Israel. In battle each God fights for his own people, and to his aid success is ascribed; Chemosh gives victory to Moab, and Asshyr to Assyria; and often the divine image or symbol accompanies the host to battle. When the ark was brought into the camp of Israel, the Philistines said,

[9] Smith *Ibid.*

> "Gods are come into the camp; who can deliver us from their own practice, for when David defeated them at Baalperazim, part of the booty consisted in their idols which had been carried into the field." When the Carthaginians, in their treaty with Phillip of Macedon, speak of "the Gods that take part in the campaign," they doubtless refer to the inmates of the sacred tent which was pitched in time of war beside the tent of the general, and before which prisoners were sacrificed after a victory. Similarly an Arabic poet says, "Yaguth went forth with us against Morad;" that is, the image of the God Yaguth was carried into the fray."

This fact had produced a solidarity between God and the community.

> "Hence, on the principle of solidarity between Gods and their worshippers, the particularism characteristic of political society could not but reappear in the sphere of religion. In the same measure as the God of a clan or town had indisputable claim to the reverence and service of the community to which he belonged, he was necessarily an enemy to their enemies and a stranger to those to whom they were strangers."[10]

God had become attached to a community, and the community had become attached to their God. God had become the God of the Community and the Community had become the chosen community of the God.

This view had two consequences. Antique Society never came to conceive that God could be universal God, the God of all. Antique Society never could conceive that there was any such thing as humanity in general.

The third point of difference between ancient and modern society, has reference to the conception of the fatherhood of God. In the antique Society God was the Father of his people but the basis of this conception of Fatherhood was deemed to be physical.

> "In heathen religions the Fatherhood of the Gods is physical fatherhood. Among the Greeks, for example, the idea that the Gods fashioned men out of clay, as potters fashion images, is relatively modern. The older conception is that the races of men have Gods for their ancestors, or are the children of the earth, the common mother of Gods and men, so that men are really of the stock or kin of the Gods. That the same conception was familiar to the older Semites appears from the Bible. Jeremiah describes idolaters as saying to a stock, Thou art my father; and to a stone, Thou hast brought me forth. In the ancient poem, Num. xxi. 29, The Moabites are called the sons and daughters of Chemosh, and at a much more recent date the prophet Malachi calls a heathen woman "the daughter of a strange God." These phrases are doubtless accommodations to the language, which the heathen neighbours of Israel used about themselves. In Syria and Palestine each clan,

[10] Smith *Ibid.*

> or even complex of clans forming a small independent people, traced back its origin to a great first father; and they indicate that, just as in Greece this father or progenitor of the race was commonly identified with the God of the race. With this it accords that in the judgment of most modern enquirers several names of deities appear in the old genealogies of nations in the Book of Genesis. Edom, for example, the progenitor of the Edomites, was identified by the Hebrews with Esau the brother of Jacob, but to the heathen he was a God, as appears from the theophorous proper name Obededom, "worshipper of Edom," the extant fragments of Phoenician and Babylonian cosmogonies date from a time when tribal religion and the connection of individual Gods with particular kindreds was forgotten or had fallen into the background. But in a generalized form the notion that men are the offspring of the Gods still held its ground. In the Phoenician cosmogony of Philo Bablius it does so in a confused shape, due to the authors euhemerism, that is, to his theory that deities are nothing more than deified men who had been great benefactors to their species. Again, in the Chaldaean legend preserved by Berosus, the belief that men are of the blood of the Gods is expressed in a form too crude not to be very ancient; for animals as well as men are said to have been formed out of clay mingled with the blood of a decapitated deity."[11]

This conception of blood kinship of Gods and men had one important consequence. To the antique world God was a human being and as such was not capable of absolute virtue and absolute goodness. God shared the physical nature of man and was afflicted with the passions infirmities and vices to which man was subject. The God of the antique world had all the wants and appetites of man and he often indulged in the vices in which many revelled. Worshipers had to implore God not to lead them into temptations.

In modern Society the idea of divine fatherhood has become entirely dissociated from the physical basis of natural fatherhood. In its place man is conceived to be created in the image of God; he is not deemed to be begotten by God. This change in the conception of the fatherhood of God looked at from its moral aspect has made a tremendous difference in the nature of God as a Governor of the Universe. God with his physical basis was not capable of absolute good and absolute virtue. With God wanting in righteousness the universe could not insist on righteousness as an immutable principle. This dissociation of God from physical contact with man has made it possible for God to be conceived of as capable of absolute good and absolute virtue.

The fourth point of difference relates to the part religion plays when a change of nationality takes place.

In the antique world there could be no change of nationality unless it was accompanied by a change of Religion. In the antique world,

[11] Smith *Ibid.*

> "It was impossible for an individual to change his religion without changing his nationality, and a whole community could hardly change its religion at all without being absorbed into another stock or nation. Religions like political ties were transmitted from father to son; for a man could not choose a new God at will; the Gods of his fathers were the only deities on whom he could count as friendly and ready to accept his homage, unless he forswore his own kindred and was received into a new circle of civil as well as religious life."

How change of religion was a condition precedent to a Social fusion is well illustrated by the dialogue between Naomi and Ruth in the Old Testament.

> "Thy Sister" says Naomi to Ruth, "is gone back unto her people and unto her Gods"; and Ruth replies, "Thy people shall be my people and thy God my God."

It is quite clear that in the ancient world a change of nationality involved a change of cult. Social fusion meant religious fusion.

In modern society abandonment of religion or acceptance of another is not necessary for social fusion. This is best illustrated by what is in modern terminology and naturalization, whereby the citizen of one state abandons his citizenship of the state and becomes a citizen of new state. In this process of naturalization religion has no place. One can have a social fusion—which is another name for naturalization—without undergoing a religious fusion.

To distinguish modern society from antique society it is not enough to say that Modern Society consists of men only. It must be added that it consists of men who are worshippers of different Gods.

The fifth point of difference relates to the necessity of knowledge as to the nature of God as part of religion.

> "From the antique point of view, indeed the question what the Gods are in themselves is not a religious but a speculative one; what is requisite to religion is a practical acquaintance with the rules on which the deity acts and on which he expects his worshippers to frame their conduct—what in 2 Kings xvii. 26 is called the "manner" or rather the "customary law" (misphat) of the God of the land. This is true even of the religion of Israel. When the prophets speak of the knowledge of the laws and principles of His government in Israel, and a summary expression for religion as a whole is "the knowledge and fear of Jehovah," i.e. the knowledge of what Jehovah prescribes, combined with a reverent obedience. An extreme skepticism towards all religious speculation is recommended in the Book of Ecclesiastes as the proper attitude of piety, for no amount of discussion can carry a man beyond the plain rule, to "fear God and keep His Commandments." This counsel the author puts into the mouth of Solomon, and so represents it, not unjustly, as summing up the old view of religion, which in

more modern days had unfortunately begun to be undermined."

The sixth point of difference relates to the place of belief in Religion.

In ancient Society:—

> "Ritual and practical usages were, strictly speaking, the sum total of ancient religions. Religion in primitive times was not a system of belief with practical applications; it was a body of fixed traditional practices, to which every member of society conformed as a matter of courage. Men would not be men if they agreed to do certain things without having a reason for their action; but in ancient religion the reason was not first formulated as a doctrine and then expressed in practice, but conversely, practice preceded doctrinal theory. Men form general rule of conduct before they begin to express general principles in words; political institutions are older than political theories and in like manner religious institutions are older than religious theories. This analogy is not arbitrarily chosen, for in fact the parallelism in ancient society between religious and political institutions is complete. In each sphere great importance was attached to form and precedent, but the explanation why the precedent was followed consisted merely of legend as to its first establishment. That the precedent, once established, was authoritative did not appear to require any proof. The rules of society were based on precedent, and the continued existence of the society was sufficient reason why a precedent once set should continue to be followed."

The seventh point of difference relates to the place of individual conviction in Religion. In ancient Society:—

> "Religion was a part of the organized social life into which a man was born, and to which he conformed through life in the same unconscious way in which men fall into any habitual practice of the society in which they live. Men took the Gods and their worship for granted, just as they took the other usages of the state for granted, and if they reason or speculated about them, they did so on the presupposition that the traditional usages were fixed things, behind which their reasoning must not go, and which no reasoning could be allowed to overturn. To us moderns religion is above all a matter of individual conviction and reasoned belief, but to the ancients it was a part of the citizen's public life, reduced to fixed forms, which he was not bound to understand and was not at liberty to criticize or to neglect. Religious non-conformity was an offence against the state; for if sacred tradition was tampered with the bases of society were undermined, and the favour of the Gods was forfeited. But so long as the prescribed forms were duly observed, a man was recognized as truly pious, and no one asked how his religion was rooted in his heart or affect-

> ed his reason. Like political duty, of which indeed it was a part, religion was entirely comprehended in the observance of certain fixed rules of outward conduct."

The eighth point of difference pertains to the relation of God to Society and man, of Society to Man in the matter of God's Providence.

First as to the difference in the relation of God to Society. In this connection three points may be noted.

The faith of the antique world

> "Sought nothing higher than a condition of physical *bien etre*. . . . The good things desired of the Gods were the blessings of earthly life, not spiritual but carnal things."

What the antique societies asked and believed themselves to receive from their God lay mainly in the following things:

> "Abundant harvests, help against their enemies and counsel by oracles or soothsayers in matters of natural difficulty."

In the antique world

> "Religion was not the affair of the individual but of the Community. . . . It was the community, and not the individual, that was sure of the permanent and the unfailing hand of the deity."

Next as to the difference in the relation of God to man.

> "It was not the business of the Gods of heathenism to watch, by a series of special providences, over the welfare of every individual. It is true that individuals laid their private affairs before the Gods, and asked with prayers and views for strictly personal blessings. But they did this just as they might crave a personal boon from a king, or as a son craves a boon from a father, without expecting to get all that was asked. What the Gods might do in this way was done as a matter of personal favour, and was no part of their proper function as heads of the community."

> "The Gods watched over a man's civic life, they gave him his share in public benefits, the annual largess of the harvest and the vintage, national peace or victory over enemies, and so forth, but they were not sure helpers in every private need, and above all they would not help him in matters that were against the interests of the community as a whole. There was therefore a whole region of possible needs and desires for which religion could and would do nothing."

Next the difference in the attitude of God and Society to man.

In the antique world Society was indifferent to individual welfare.

God was no doubt bound to Society. But

> "The compact between the God and his worshippers was not

> held to pledge the deity to make the private cares of each member of the Community his own."
>
> "The benefits expected of God were of a public character affecting the whole community, especially fruitful seasons, increase of flocks of herds and success in war. So long as community flourished the fact that an individual was miserable reflected no discredit on divine providence."

On the contrary the antique world looked upon the misery of a man as proof.

> "That the sufferer was an evil-doer, justly hateful to the Gods. Such a man was out of place among the happy and the prosperous crowd that assembled on feast days before the alter."

It is in accordance with this view that the leper and the mourner were shut out from the exercise of religion as well as from the privileges of social life and their food was not brought into the house of God.

As for conflict between individual and individual and between society and the individual God had no concern. In the antique world:

> "It was not expected that (God) should always be busy righting human affairs. In ordinary matters it was men's business to help themselves and their own kins folk, though the sense that the God was always near, and could be called upon at need, was a moral force continually working in some degree for the maintenance of social righteousness and order. The strength of this moral force was indeed very uncertain, for it was always possible for the evil-doer to flatter himself that his offence would be overlooked."

In the antique world man did not ask God to be righteous to him.

> "Whether in civil or in profane matters, the habit of the old world was to think much of the community and little of the individual life, and no one felt this to be unjust even though it bore hardly on himself. The God was the God of the national or of the tribe, and he knew and cared for the individual only as a member of the community."

That was the attitude that man in the antique world took of his own private misfortune. Man came to rejoice before his God and

> "in rejoicing before his God man rejoiced with and for the welfare of his kindred, his neighbours and his country, and, in renewing by a solemn act of worship the bond that united him to God, he also renewed the bonds of family, social and national obligation."

Man in the antique world did not call upon his maker to be righteous to him.

Such is this other Revolution in Religion.

There have thus been two Religious Revolutions. One was an external Revolution. The other was an internal Revolution. The External Revolution was concerned with the field within which the authority of Religion was to prevail. The Internal Revolution had to do with the changes in Religion as a scheme of divine Governance for human society. The External Revolution was not really a Religious Revolution at all. It was a revolt of science against the extra territorial jurisdiction assumed by Religion over a field which did not belong. The Internal Revolution was a real Revolution or may be compared to any other political Revolution, such as the French Revolution or the Russian Revolution. It involved a constitutional change. By this Revolution the Scheme of divine governance came to be altered, amended and reconstituted.

How profound have been the changes which this internal Revolution, has made in the antique scheme of divine governance can be easily seen. By this Revolution God has ceased to be a member of a community. Thereby he has become impartial. God has ceased to be the Father of Man in the physical sense of the word. He has become the creator of the Universe. The breaking of this blood bond has made it possible to hold that God is good. By this Revolution man has ceased to be a blind worshipper of God doing nothing but obeying his commands. Thereby man has become a responsible person required to justify his belief in God's commandments by his conviction. By this Revolution God has ceased to be merely the protector of Society and social interests in gross have ceased to be the center of the divine Order. Society and man have changed places as centers of this divine order. It is man who has become the center of it.

All this analysis of the Revolution in the Ruling concepts of Religion as a scheme of divine governance had one purpose namely to discover the norm for evaluating the philosophy of a Religion. The impatient reader may not ask where are these norms and what are they? The reader may not have found the norms specified by their names in the foregoing discussion. But he could not have failed to notice that the whole of this Religious Revolution was raging around the norms for judging what is right and what is wrong. If he has not, let me make explicit what has been implicit in the whole of this discussion. We began with the distinction between antique society and modern society as has been pointed out they differed in the type of divine governance they accepted as their Religious ideals. At one end of the Revolution was the antique society with its Religious ideal in which the end was Society. At the other end of the Revolution is the modern Society with its Religious ideal in which the end is the individual. To put the same fact in terms of the norm it can be said that the norm or the criterion, for judging right and wrong in the Antique Society was *utility* while the norm or the criterion for judging right and wrong in the modern Society is *Justice*. The Religious Revolution was not thus a revolution in the religious organization of Society resulting in the shifting of the center—from society to the individual—it was a revolution in the norms.

Some may demur to the norms I have suggested. It may be that it is a new way of reaching them. But to my mind there is no doubt that they are the real norms by which to judge the philosophy of religion. In the first place the norm must enable people to judge what is right and wrong in the conduct of men. In the second place the norm must be appropriate to current notion of what constitutes the moral good. From both these points of view they appear to be the true norms. They enable us to judge what is right and wrong. They are appropriate to the society which adopted them. Utility as a criterion was appropriate to the antique world in which society being the end, the moral good was held to be something which had social utility. Justice as a criterion became appropriate to the Modern World in which individual being the end, the moral good was held to be something which does justice to the individual. There may be controversy as to which of the two norms is morally superior. But I do not think there can be any serious controversy that these are not the norms. If it is said that these norms are not transcendental enough; my reply is that if a norm whereby one is to judge the philosophy of religion must be Godly, it must also be earthly. At any rate these are the norms I propose to adopt in examining the philosophy of Hinduism.

II.

This is a long detour. But it was a necessary preliminary to any inquiry into the main question. However, when one begins the inquiry one meets with an initial difficulty. The Hindu is not prepared to face the inquiry. He either argues that religion is of no importance or he takes shelter behind the view—fostered by the study of comparative Religion—that all religions are good. There is no doubt that both these views are mistaken and untenable.

Religion as a social force cannot be ignored. Religion has been aptly described by Hebert Spencer as "the weft which everywhere crosses the warp of history." This is true of every Society. But Religion has not only crossed everywhere the warp of Indian History it forms the warp and woof of the Hindu mind. The life of the Hindu is regulated by Religion at every moment of his life. It orders him how during life he should conduct himself and how on death his body shall be disposed of. It tells him how and when he shall indulge in his sexual impulses. It tells him what ceremonies are to be performed when a child is born—how he should name, how he should cut the hair on its head, how he should perform its first feeding. It tells him what occupation he can take to, what woman he should marry. It tells him with whom he should dine and what food he should eat, what vegetables are lawful and what are forbidden. It tells how he should spend his day, how many times he should eat, how many times he should pray. There is no act of the Hindu which is not covered or ordained by Religion. It seems strange that the educated Hindus should come to look upon it as though it was a matter of indifference.

Besides, Religion is a social force. As I have pointed out Religion stands for a scheme of divine governance. The scheme becomes an ideal for society to follow. The ideal may be non-existent in the sense that it is something which is constructed. But although non-existent, it is real. For an ideal it has full operative force which is inherent in every ideal. Those who deny the importance of religion not only forget this, they also fail to realize how great is the potency and sanction that lies behind a religious ideal as compound with that of a purely secular ideal. This is probably due to the lag which one sees between the real and the ideal which is always present whether the ideal is religious or secular. But the relative potency of the two ideals is to be measured by another test—namely their power to override the practical instincts of man. The ideal is concerned with something that is remote. The practical instincts of man are concerned with the immediate present. Now placed as against the force of the practical instincts of man the two ideals show their difference in an unmistaken manner. The practical instincts of man do yield to the prescriptions of a religious ideal however much the two are opposed to each other. The practical instincts of man do not on the other hand yield to the secular ideal if the two are in conflict. This means that a religious ideal has a hold on mankind, irrespective of an earthly gain. This can never be said of a purely secular ideal. Its power depends upon its power to confer material benefit. This shows how great is the difference in the potency and sanction of the two ideals over the human mind. A religious ideal never fails to work so long as there is faith in that ideal. To ignore religion is to ignore a live wire.

Again to hold that all religions are true and good is to cherish a belief which is positively and demonstrably wrong. This belief, one is sorry to say, is the result of what is known as the study of comparative religion. Comparative religion has done one great service to humanity. It has broken down the claim and arrogance of revealed religions as being the only true and good religions of study. While it is true that comparative religion has abrogated the capricious distinction between true and false religions based on purely arbitrary and a priori considerations, it has brought in its wake some false notions about religion. The most harmful one is the one I have mentioned namely that all religions are equally good and that there is no necessity of discriminating between them. Nothing can be a greater error than this. Religion is an institution or an influence and like all social influences and institutions, it may help or it may harm a society which is in its grip. As pointed out by Prof. Tiele[12] religion is

> "one of the mightiest motors in the history of mankind, which formed as well as tore asunder nations, united as well as divided empires, which sanctioned the most atrocious and barbarous deeds, the most libinous customs, inspired the most admirable acts of heroism, self renunciation, and devotion, which occasioned the most sanguinary wars, rebellions and persecutions, as well as brought about the freedom, happiness and peace of nations—at one time a partisan of tyranny, at another breaking its chains, now calling into existence and fostering a new and brilliant civilization, then the deadly foe to progress, science and art."

A force which shows such a strange contrast in its result can be accepted as good without examining the form it takes and the ideal it serves. Everything depends upon what social ideal a given religion as a divine scheme of governance hold out. This is a question which is not avowed by the science of comparative religion. Indeed it begins where comparative religion ends. The Hindu is merely trying to avoid it by saying that although religions are many they are equally good. For they are not.

However much the Hindu may seek to burke the inquiry into the philosophy of Hinduism there is no escape. He must face it.

[12] Quoted by Crowby, Tree of Life, page 5.

III.

Now to begin with the subject. I propose to apply both the tests, the test of justice and the test of utility to judge the philosophy of Hinduism. First I will apply the test of justice. Before doing so I want to explain what I mean by the principle of justice. No one has expounded it better than Professor Bergbon.[13] As interpreted by him the principle of justice is a compendious one and includes most of the other principles which have become the foundation of a moral order. Justice has always evoked ideas of equality, of proportion of "compensation." Equity signifies equality. Rules and regulations, right and righteousness are concerned with equality in value. If all men are equal, all men are of the same essence and the common essence entitled them to the same fundamental rights and to equal liberty.

In short justice is simply another name for liberty equality and fraternity. It is in this sense I shall be using[14] justice as a criterion to judge Hinduism.

Which of these tenets does Hinduism recognize? Let us take the question one by one.

I. Does Hinduism recognize Equality?

The question instantaneously brings to one's mind the caste system. One striking feature of the caste system is that the different castes do not stand as an horizontal series all on the same plane. It is a system in which the different castes are placed in a vertical series one above the other. Manu may not be responsible for the creation of caste. Manu preached the sanctity of the Varna and as I have shown Varna is the parent of caste. In that sense Manu can be charged with being the progenitor if not the author of the Caste System. Whatever be the case as to the guilt of Manu regarding the Caste System there can be no question that Manu is responsible for upholding the principle of gradation and rank.

In the scheme of Manu the Brahmin is placed at the first in rank. *Below* him is the Kshatriya. *Below* Kshatriya is the Vaishya. *Below* Vaishya is the Shudra and *Below* Shudra is the Ati-Shudra (the Untouchables). This system of rank and gradation is, simply another way of enunciating the principle of inequality so that it may be truly said that Hinduism does not recognize equality. This inequality in status is not merely the inequality that one sees in the warrant of precedence prescribed for a ceremonial gathering at a King's Court. It is a permanent social relationship among the classes to be observed— to be enforced—at all times in all places and for all purposes. It will take too long to show how in every phase of life Manu has introduced and made inequality the vital force of life. But I will illustrate it by taking a few examples such as slavery, marriage and Rule of Law.

Manu recognizes[15] Slavery. But he confined it to the Shudras. Only Shudras could be made slaves of the three higher classes. But the higher classes could not be the slaves of the Shudra.

---

[13] Two Moralities page.

[14] For another interpretation of justice, *see*, J. S. Mill—Utilitarianism.

[15] Manu recognizes seven kinds of slaves (VIII-415). Narada recognizes fifteen kinds of slaves (V-25).

But evidently practice differed from the law of Manu and not only Shudras happened to become slaves but members of the other three classes also become slaves. When this was discovered to be the case a new rule was enacted by a Successor of Manu namely Narada.[16] This new rule of Narada runs as follows:—

> V. 39. "In the inverse order of the four castes slavery is not ordained except where a man violates the duties peculiar to his caste. Slavery (in that respect) is analogous to the condition of a wife."

Recognition of slavery was bad enough. But if the rule of slavery had been left free to take its own course it would have had at least one beneficial effect. It would have been a levelling force. The foundation of caste would have been destroyed. For under it a Brahmin might have become the slave of the Untouchable and the Untouchable would have become the master of the Brahmin. But it was seen that unfettered slavery was an equalitarian principle and an attempt was made to nullify it. Manu and his successors therefore while recognizing slavery ordain that it shall not be recognized in its inverse order to the Varna System. That means that a Brahmin may become the slave of another Brahmin. But he shall not be the slave of a person of another Varna i.e. of the Kshatriya, Vaishya, Shudra, or Ati-Shudra. On the other hand a Brahmin may hold as his slave any one belonging to the four Varnas. A Kshatriya can have a Kshatriya, Vaisha, Shudra and Ati-Shudra as his slaves but not one who is a Brahmin. A Vaishya can have a Vaishya, Shudra and Ati-Shudra as his slaves but not one who is a Brahmin or a Kshatriya. A Shudra can hold a Shudra and Ati-shudra can hold an Ati-Shudra as his slave but not one who is a Brahmin, Kshatriya, Vaishya or Shudra.

Consider Manu on marriage. Here are his rules governing intermarriage among the different classes.

Manu says:—

> III. 12. "For the first marriage of the twice born classes, a woman of the same class is recommended but for such as are impelled by inclination to marry again, women in the direct order of the classes are to be preferred."
>
> III. 13. "A Shudra woman only must be the wife of Shudra: she and a Vaisya, of a Vaisya; they two and a Kshatriya, of a Kshatriya; those two and a Brahmani of a Brahman."

Manu is of course opposed to intermarriage. His injunction is for each class to marry within his class. But he does recognize marriage outside the defined class. Here again he is particularly careful not to allow intermarriage to do harm to his principle of inequality among classes. Like Slavery he permits intermarriage but not in the inverse order. A Brahmin when marrying outside his class may marry any woman from any of the classes below him. A Kshatriya is free to marry a woman from the two classes next below him namely the Vaishya and Shudra but must not marry a woman from the Brahmin class which is above him. A Vaishya

[16] The same rule is laid down by Yajnavalkya (II-183) whose authority is equal to that of Manu.

is free to marry a woman from the Shudra Class which is next below him. But he cannot marry a woman from the Brahmin and the Kshatriya Class which are above him.

Why this discrimination? The only answer is that Manu was most anxious to preserve the rule of inequality which was his guiding principle.

Take Rule of Law. Rule of Law is generally understood to mean equality before law. Let any one interested to know what Manu has to say on the point ponder over the following Rules extracted from his code which for easy understanding I have arranged under distinct headings.

As to witnesses.—According to Manu they are to be sworn as follows:—

> VIII. 87. "In the forenoon let the judge, being purified, severally call on the twice-born, being purified also, to declare the truth, in the presence of some image, a symbol of the divinity and of Brahmins, while the witnesses turn their faces either to the north or to the east."

> VIII. 88. "To a Brahman he must begin with saying, `Declare'; to a Kshatriya, with saying, 'Declare the truth'; to a Vaisya, with comparing perjury to the crime of stealing kine, grain or gold; to a Sudra, with comparing it in some or all of the following sentences, to every crime that men can commit."

> VIII. 113. "Let the judge cause a priest to swear by his veracity; a soldier, by his horse, or elephant, and his weapons; a merchant, by his kine, grain, and gold; a mechanic or servile man, by imprecating on his own head, if he speak falsely, all possible crimes."

Manu also deals with cases of witnesses giving false evidence. According to Manu giving false evidence is a crime, says Manu:—

> VIII. 122. "Learned men have specified these punishments, which were ordained by sage legislators for perjured witnesses, with a view to prevent a failure of justice and to restrain iniquity."

> VIII. 123. "Let a just prince banish men of the three lower classes, if they give false evidence, having first levied the fine; but a Brahman let him only banish."

But Manu made one exception:—

> VIII. 112. "To women, however, at a time of dalliance, or on a proposal of marriage, in the case of grass or fruit eaten by a cow, of wood taken for a sacrifice, or of a promise made for the preservation of a Brahman, it is deadly sin to take a light oath."

As parties to proceedings—Their position can be illustrated by quoting the ordinances of Manu relating to a few of the important criminal offences dealt with by Manu.

Take the offence of Defamation. Manu says:—

VIII. 267. "A soldier, defaming a priest, shall be fined a hundred panas, a merchant, thus offending, an hundred and fifty, or two hundred; but, for such an offence, a mechanic or servile man shall be shipped."

VIII. 268. "A priest shall be fined fifty, if he slander a soldier; twenty five, if a merchant; and twelve, if he slander a man of the servile class."

Take the offence of Insult—Manu says:—

VIII. 270. "A once born man, who insults the twice-born with gross invectives, ought to have his tongue slit; for he sprang from the lowest part of Brahma."

VIII. 271. "If he mention their names and classes with contumely, as if he say, "Oh Devadatta, though refuse of Brahmin," an iron style, ten fingers long, shall be thrust red into his mouth."

VIII. 272. "Should he, through pride, give instruction to priests concerning their duty, let the king order some hot oil to be dropped into his mouth and his ear."

Take the offence of Abuse—Manu says:—

VIII. 276. "For mutual abuse by a priest and a soldier, this fine must be imposed by a learned king; the lowest amercement on the priest, and the middle-most on the soldier."

VIII. 277. "Such exactly, as before mentioned, must be the punishment a merchant and a mechanic, in respect of their several classes, except the slitting of the tongue; this is a fixed rule of punishment."

Take the offence of Assault—Manu propounds:—

VIII. 279. "With whatever member a low-born man shall assault or hurt a superior, even that member of his must be slit, or cut more or less in proportion to the injury; this is an ordinance of Manu."

VIII. 280. "He who raises his hand or a staff against another, shall have his hand cut; and he, who kicks another in wrath, shall have an incision made in his foot."

Take the offence of Arrogance—According to Manu:—

VIII. 281. "A man of the lowest class, who shall insolently place himself on the same seat with one of the highest, shall either be banished with a mark on his hinder parts, or the king, shall cause a gash to be made on his buttock."

VIII. 282. "Should he spit on him through price, the king shall order both his lips to be gashed; should he urine on him, his penis: should he break wing against him, his anus."

VIII. 283. "If he seize the Brahman by the locks, or by the feet, or by the beard, or by the throat, or by the scrotum, let the king without hesitation cause incisions to be made in his hands."

Take the offence of Adultery. Says Manu:—

VIII. 359. "A man of the servile class, who commits actual adultery with the wife of a priest, ought to suffer death; the wives, indeed, of all the four classes must ever be most especially guarded."

VIII. 366. "A low man, who makes love to a damsel of high birth, ought to be punished corporally; but he who addresses a maid of equal rank, shall give the nuptial present and marry her, if her father please."

VIII. 374. "A mechanic or servile man, having an adulterous connection with a woman of a twice-born class, whether guarded at home or unguarded, shall thus be punished; if she was unguarded, he shall lose the part offending, and his whole substance; if guarded, and a priestess, every thing, even his life."

VIII. 375. "For adultery with a guarded priestess, a merchant shall forfeit all his wealth after imprisonment for a year; a soldier shall be fined a thousand panas, and he be shaved with the urine of an ass."

VIII. 376. "But, if a merchant or soldier commit adultery with a woman of the sacerdotal class, whom her husband guards not at home, the king shall only fine the merchant five hundred, and the soldier a thousand:"

VIII. 377. "Both of them, however, if they commit that offence with a priestess not only guarded but eminent for good qualities, shall be punished like men of the servile class, or be burned in a fire of dry grass or reeds."

VIII. 382. "If a merchant converse criminally with a guarded woman of the military, or a soldier with one of the mercantile class, they both deserve the same punishment as in the case of a priestess unguarded."

VIII. 383. "But a Brahman, who shall commit adultery with a guarded woman of those two classes, must be fined a thousand panas; and for the life offence with a guarded woman of the servile class, the fine of a soldier or a merchant shall be also one thousand."

VIII. 384. "For adultery with a woman of the military class, if guarded, the fine of a merchant is five hundred; but a soldier, for the converse of that offence, must be shaved with urine, or pay the fine just mentioned."

VIII. 385. "A priest shall pay five hundred panas if he connect himself criminally with an unguarded woman of the military, commercial, or servile class, and a thousand, for such a connexion with a woman of a vile mixed breed."

Turning to the system of punishment for offences Manu's Scheme throws an interesting light on the subject. Consider the following ordinances:—

VIII. 379. "Ignominious tonsure is ordained, instead of capital punishment, for an adulterer of the priestly class, where the punishment of other classes may extend to loss of life."

VIII. 380. "Never shall the king slay a Brahman, though convicted of all possible crimes; let him banish the offender from his realm, but with all his property secure, and his body unhurt."

XI. 127. "For killing intentionally a virtuous man of the military class, the penance must be a fourth part of that ordained for killing a priest; for killing a Vaisya, only an eighth, for killing a Sudra, who had been constant in discharging his duties, a sixteenth part."

XI. 128. "But, if a Brahmen kill a Kshatriya without malice, he must, after a full performance of his religious rites, give the priests one bull together with a thousand cows."

XI. 129. "Or he may perform for three years the penance for slaying a Brahmen, mortifying his organs of sensation and action, letting his hair grow long, and living remote from the town, with the root of a tree for his mansion."

XI. 130. "If he kill without malice a Vaisya, who had a good moral character, he may perform the same penance for one year, or give the priests a hundred cows and a bull."

XI. 131. "For six months must he perform this whole penance, if without intention he kill a Sudra; or he may give ten white cows and a bull to the priests."

VIII. 381. "No greater crime is known on earth than slaying a Brahman; and the king, therefore, must not even form in his mind an idea of killing a priest."

VIII. 126. "Let the king having considered and ascertained the frequency of a similar offence, the place and time, the ability of the criminal to pay or suffer and the crime itself, cause punishment to fall on those alone, who deserves it."

VIII. 124. "Manu, son of the Self-existent, has named ten places of punishment, which are appropriated to the three lower classes, but a Brahman must depart from the realm unhurt in any one of them."

VIII. 125. "The part of generation, the belly, the tongue, the two hands, and, fifthly, the two feet, the eye, the nose, both ears, the property, and, in a capital case, the whole body."

How strange is the contrast between Hindu and Non-Hindu criminal jurisprudence? How inequality is writ large in Hinduism as seen in its criminal jurisprudence? In a penal code charged with the spirit of justice we find two things—a section dealing defining the crime and a section prescribing a rational form of punishment for breach of it and a rule that all offenders are liable to the same penalty. In Manu what do we find? First an irrational system of punishment. The punishment for a crime is inflicted on the organ concerned in the crime such as belly, tongue, nose, eyes, ears, organs of generation etc., as if the offending organ was a sentient being having a will for its own and had not been merely a servitor of human being. Second feature of Manu's penal code is the inhuman character of the punishment which has no proportion to the gravity of the offence. But the most striking feature of Manu's Penal Code which stands out in all its nakedness is the inequality of punishment for the same offence. Inequality designed not merely to punish the offender but to protect also the dignity and to maintain the baseness of the parties coming to a Court of Law to seek justice in other words to maintain the social inequality on which his whole scheme is founded.

So far I have taken for illustrations such matters as serve to show how Manu has ordained social inequality. I now propose to take other matters dealt with by Manu in order to illustrate that Manu has also ordained Religious inequality. These are matters which are connected with what are called sacraments and Ashrams.

The Hindus like the Christians believe in sacraments. The only difference is that the Hindus have so many of them that even the Roman Catholic Christians would be surprised at the extravagant number observed by the Hindus. Originally their number was forty and covered the most trivial as well as the most important occasions in a person's life. First they were reduced to twenty. Later on it was reduced to sixteen[17] and at that figure the sacraments of the Hindus have remained stabilized.

Before I explain how at the core of these rules of sacraments there lies the spirit of inequality the reader must know what the rules are. It is impossible to examine all. It will be enough if I deal with a few of them. I will take only three categories of them, those relating with Initiation, Gayatri and Daily Sacrifices.

First as to Initiation. This initiation is effected by the investitute of a person with the sacred thread. The following are the most important rules of Manu regarding the sacrament of investitute.

> II. 36. "In the eighth year from the conception of a Brahman, in the eleventh from that of a Kshatriya, and in the twelfth from that of a Vaisya, let the father invest the child with the mark of his class."
>
> II. 37. "Should a Brahman, or his father for him, be desirous of his advancement in sacred knowledge; a Kshatriya, of extend-

[17] The following are the sixteen sacraments.

> ing his power; or a Vaisya of engaging in mercantile business; the investitute may be made in the fifth, sixth, or eighth years respectively."
>
> II. 38. "The ceremony of investitute hallowed by the Gayatri must not be delayed, in the case of a priest, beyond the sixteenth year; nor in that of a soldier, beyond the twenty second; nor in that of a merchant, beyond the twenty fourth."
>
> II. 39. "After that, all youths of these three classes, who have not been invested at the proper time, become vratyas, or outcasts, degraded from the Gayatri, and condemned by the virtuous."
>
> II. 147. "Let a man consider that as a mere human birth, which his parents gave him for their mutual gratification, and which he receives after lying in the womb."
>
> II. 148. "But that birth which his principal acharya, who knows the whole Veda, procures for him by his divine mother the Gayatri, is a true birth; that birth is exempt from age and from death."
>
> II. 169. "The first birth is from a natural mother; the second, from the ligation of the zone; the third from the due performance of the sacrifice; such are the births of him who is usually called twice-born, according to a text of the Veda."
>
> II. 170. "Among them his divine birth is that, which is distinguished by the ligation of the zone, and sacrificial cord; and in that birth the Gayatri is his mother, and the Acharya, his father."

Then let me come to Gayatri. It is a Mantra or an invocation of special spiritual efficacy. Manu explains what it is.

> II. 76. "Brahma milked out, as it were, from the three Vedas, the letter A, the letter U, and the letter M which form by their coalition the triliteral monosyllable, together with three mysterious words, bhur, bhuvah, swer, or earth, sky, heaven."
>
> II. 77. "From the three Vedas, also the Lord of creatures, incomprehensibly exalted, successively milked out the three measures of that ineffable text, be ginning with the word tad, and entitled Savitri or Gayatri."
>
> II. 78. "A priest who shall know the Veda, and shall pronounce to himself, both morning and evening, that syllable and that holy text preceded by the three words, shall attain the sanctity which the Veda confers."
>
> II. 79. "And a twice born man, who shall a thousand times repeat those three (or om, the vyahritis, and the gayatri,) apart from the multitude, shall be released in a month even from a great offence, as a snake from his slough."

II. 80. "The priest, the soldier, and the merchant, who shall neglect this mysterious text, and fail to perform in due season his peculiar acts of piety, shall meet with contempt among the virtuous."

II. 81 "The great immutable words, preceded by the triliteral syllable, and followed by the Gayatri which consists of three measures, must be considered as the mouth, or principal part of the Veda."

II. 82. "Whoever shall repeat, day by day, for three years, without negligence, that sacred text, shall hereafter approach the divine essence, move as freely as air, and assume an ethereal form."

II. 83. "The triliteral monosyllable is an emblem of the Supreme, the suppressions of breath with a mind fixed on God are the highest devotion; but nothing is more exalted than the gayatri; a declaration of truth is more excellent than silence."

II. 84. "All rights ordained in the Veda, oblations to fire, and solemn sacrifices pass away; but that which passes not away, is declared to be the sylable om, thence called acshare; since it is a symbol of God, the Lord of created beings."

II. 85. "The act of repeating his Holy Name is ten times better than the appointed sacrifice; an hundred times better when it is heard by no man; and a thousand times better when it is purely mental."

II. 86. "The four domestic sacraments which are accompanied with the appointed sacrifice, are not equal, though all be united, to a sixteenth part of the sacrifice performed by a repetition of the gayatri."

Now to the Daily Sacrifices.

III. 69. "For the sake of expiating offences committed ignorantly in those places mentioned in order, the five great sacrifices were appointed by eminent sages to be performed each day by such as keep house."

III. 70. "Teaching (and studying) the scripture is the sacrifice to the Veda; offering cakes and water, the sacrifice to the Manes, an oblation to fire, the sacrifice to the Deities; giving rice or other food to living creatures, the sacraments of spirits; receiving guests with honour, the sacrifice to men."

III. 71. "Whoever omits not those five great sacrifices, if he has ability to perform them, is untainted by the sons of the five slaughtering places, even though he constantly resides at home."

Turning to the Ashramas. The Ashram theory is a peculiar feature of the philosophy of Hinduism. It is not known to have found a place in the teachings of any other religion. According to the Ashram theory life is to be divided into four stages called *Brahmachari, Grahastha, Vanaprastha* and *Sannyas*. In the Brahamachari stage a person is unmarried and devotes his time to the study and education. After this stage is over he enters the stage of a Grahastha i.e. he marries, rears a family and attends to his worldly welfare. Thereafter he enters the third stage and is then known as a Vanaprastha. As a Vanaprastha he dwells in the forest as a hermit but without severing his ties with his family or without abandoning his rights to his worldly goods. Then comes the fourth and the last stage—that of Sannyas—which means complete renunciation of the world in search of God. The two stages of Brahamchari and Grahastha are natural enough. The two last stages are only recommendatory. There is no compulsion about them. All that Manu lays down is as follows:

> VI. 1. A twice born who has thus lived according to the law in the order of householders, may, taking a firm resolution and keeping his organs in subjection, dwell in the forest, duly (observing the rules given below).
>
> VI. 2. When a householder sees his (skin) wrinkled, and (his hair) white, and the sons of his son, then he may resort to the forest.
>
> VI. 3. Abandoning all food raised by cultivation, all his belongings, he may depart into the forest, either committing his wife to his sons, or accompanied by her.
>
> VI. 33. But having passed the third part of (a man's natural term of) life in the forest, he may live as an ascetic during the fourth part of his existence, after abandoning all attachment to worldly objects.

The inequality embodied in these rules is real although it may not be quite obvious. Observe that all these sacraments and Ashramas are confined to the twice-born. The Shudras are excluded[18] from their benefit. Manu of course has no objection to their undergoing the forms of the ceremonies. But he objects to their use of the Sacred Mantras in the performance of the ceremonies. On this Manu says:—

> X. 127. "Even Shudras, who were anxious to perform their entire duty, and knowing what they should perform, imitate the practice of good men in the household sacraments, but without any holy text, except those containing praise and salutation, are so far from sinning, that they acquire just applause."

See the following text of Manu for women:—

> II. 66. "The same ceremonies, except that of the sacrificial thread, must be duly performed for women at the same age and in the same order, that the body may be made perfect; but without any text from the Veda."

[18] So also are the women.

Why does Manu prohibit the Shudras from the benefit of the Sacraments? His interdict against the Shudras becoming a Sannyasi is a puzzle. Sannyas means and involves renunciation, abandonment of worldly object. In legal language Sannyas is interpreted as being equivalent to civil death. So that when a man becomes a Sannyasi he is treated as being dead from that moment and his heir succeeds immediately. This would be the only consequence, which would follow if a Shudra become a Sannyasi. Such a consequence could hurt nobody except the Shudra himself. Why then this interdict? The issue is important and I will quote Manu to explain the significance and importance of the Sacraments and Sannyas. Let us all ponder over the following relevant texts of Manu:

> II. 26. With holy rites, prescribed by the Veda, must the ceremony on conception and other sacraments be performed for twice-born men, which sanctify the body and purify (from sin) in this (life) and after death.
>
> II. 28. By the study of the Veda, by vows, by burnt oblations, by (the recitation of) sacred texts, by the (acquisition of the) three sacred Vedas, by offering (to the gods Rishis and Manes), by (the procreation of) sons, by the Great Sacrifices, and by (Srauta) rites this (human) body is made fit for (union with) Bramha.

This is the aim and object of the Samscaras. Manu also explains the aim and object of Sannyas.

> VI. 81. He (the Sannyasi) who has in this manner gradually given up all attachments and is freed from all the pairs (of opposites), reposes in Brahman alone.
>
> VI. 85. A twice born man who becomes an ascetic, after the successive performance of the above-mentioned acts, shakes off sin here below and reaches the highest Brahman.

From these texts it is clear that according to Manu himself the object of the sacraments is to sanctify the body and purify it from sin in this life and hereafter and to make it fit for union with God. According to Manu the object of Sannyas to reach and repose in God. Yet Manu says that the sacraments and Sannyas are the privileges of the higher classes. They are not open to the Shudra. Why? Does not a Shudra need sanctification of his body, purification of his soul? Does not a Shudra need to have an aspiration to reach God? Manu probably would have answered these questions in the affirmative. Why did he then make such rules. The answer is that he was a staunch believer in social inequality and he knew the danger of admitting religious Equality. If I am equal before God why am I not equal on earth? Manu was probably terrified by this question. Rather than admit and allow religious equality to affect social inequality he preferred to deny religious equality.

Thus in Hinduism you will find both social inequality and religious inequality imbedded in its philosophy.

To prevent man from purifying himself from sin!! To prevent man from getting near to God!! To any rational person such rules must appear to be abominal and an indication of a perverse mind. It is a glaring instance of how Hinduism is a denial not only of equality but how it is denial of the sacred character of human personality.

This is not all. For Manu does not stop with the non-recognition of human personality. He advocates a deliberate debasement of human personality. I will take only two instances to illustrate this feature of the philosophy of Hinduism.

All those who study the Caste System are naturally led to inquire into the origin of it. Manu being the progenitor of Caste had to give an explanation of the origin of the various castes. What is the origin which Manu gives? His explanation is simple. He says that leaving aside the four original castes the rest are simply baseborn!! He says they are the progeny of fornication and adultery between men and women of the four original castes. The immorality and looseness of character among men and women of the four original castes must have been limitless to account for the rise of innumerable castes consisting of innumerable souls!! Manu makes the wild allegation without stopping to consider what aspersions he is casting upon men and women of the four original castes. For if the chandals—the old name for the Untouchables—are the progeny of a Brahman female and a Shudra male then it is obvious that to account for such a large number of Chandals it must be assumed that every Brahman woman was slut and a whore and every Shudra lived an adulterous life with complete abandon. Manu in his mad just for debasing the different castes by ascribing to them an ignoble origin seems deliberately to pervert historical facts. I will give only two illustrations. Take Manu's origin of *Magadha* and *Vaidehik* and compare it with the origin of the same castes as given by Panini the great Grammarian. Manu says that *Magadha* is a caste which is born from sexual intercourse between Vaishya male and Kshatriya female. Manu says that *Vaidehik* is a caste which is born from sexual intercourse between a Vaishya male and a Brahmin female. Now turn to Panini. Panini says that *Magadha* means a person who is resident of the country known as *Magadha*. As to *Vaidehik* Panini says that *Vaidehik* means a person who is resident of the country known as *Videha*. What a contrast!! How cruel it is. Panini lived not later than 300 B.C. Manu lived about 200 A.D. How is it that people who bore no stigma in the time of Panini became so stained in the hands of Manu? The answer is that Manu was bent on debasing them. Why Manu was bent on deliberately debasing people is a task which is still awaiting exploration[19] In the meantime we have the strange contrast that while Religion everywhere else is engaged in the task of raising and ennobling mankind Hinduism is busy in debasing and degrading it.

The other instance I want to use for illustrating the spirit of debasement which is inherent in Hinduism pertains to rules regarding the naming of a Hindu child.

The names among Hindus fall into four classes. They are either connected with *(i)* family deity *(ii)* the month in which the child is born *(iii)* with the planets under which a child is born or *(iv)* are purely temporal i.e. connected with business. According to Manu the temporal name of a Hindu should consist of two parts and Manu gives directions as to what the first and the second part should denote. The

[19] See my Essay "Manu on Caste—A puzzle." (*This Essay has not been found in the papers received.*—Editors.)

second part of a Brahmin's name shall be a word implying happiness; of a Kshatriya's a word implying protection; of a Vaishya's a term expressive of prosperity and of a Shudra's an expression denoting service. Accordingly the Brahmins have *Sharma* (happiness) or *Deva* (God), the Kshatriyas have *Raja* (authority) or Verma (armour), the Vaishyas have Gupta (gifts) or Datta (Giver) and the Shudras have *Das* (service) for the second part of their names. As to the first part of their names Manu says that in the case of a Brahmin it should denote something auspicious, in the case of a Kshatriya something connected with power, in the case of a Vaishya something connected with wealth. But in the case of a Shudra Manu says the first part of his name should denote something contemptible!! Those who think that such a philosophy is incredible would like to know the exact reference. For their satisfaction I am reproducing the following texts from Manu. Regarding the naming ceremony Manu says:—

> II. 30. Let (the father perform or) cause to be performed the namadheya (the rite of naming the child), on the tenth or twelfth (day after birth), or on a lucky lunar day, in a lucky muhurta under an auspicious constellation.
>
> II. 31. Let (the first part of) a Brahman's name (denote) something auspicious, a Kshatriya's name be connected with power, and a Vaishya's with wealth, but a Shudra's (express something) contemptible.
>
> II. 32. (The second part of) a Brahman's (name) shall be (a word) implying happiness, of a Kshatriya's (a word) implying protection, of a Vaishya's (a term) expressive of thriving, and of a Shudra's (an expression) denoting service.

Manu will not tolerate the Shudra to have the comfort of a high sounding name. He must be contemptible both in fact and in name.

Enough has been said to show how Hinduism is a denial of equality both social as well as religious and how it is also a degradation of human personality.

Does Hinduism recognize liberty?

Liberty to be real must be accompanied by certain social conditions.[20]

In the first place there should be social equality. "Privilege tilts the balance of social action in favour of its possessors. The more equal are the social rights of citizens, the more able they are to utilize their freedom... If liberty is to move to its appointed end it is important that there should be equality."

In the second place there must be economic security. "A man may be free to enter any vocation he may choose. . . . Yet if he is deprived of security in employment he becomes a prey of mental and physical servitude incompatible with the very essence of liberty.... The perpetual fear of the morrow, its haunting sense of impending disaster, its fitful search for happiness and beauty which perpetually eludes, shows that without economic security, liberty is not worth having. Men

[20] See Laski—Liberty in the Modern State.

may well be free and yet remain unable to realize the purposes of freedom."

In the third place there must be knowledge made available to all. In the complex world man lives at his peril and he must find his way in it without losing his freedom.

> "There can, under these conditions, be no freedom that is worthwhile unless the mind is trained to use its freedom. (Given this fact) the right of man to education becomes fundamental to his freedom. Deprive a man of knowledge and you will make him inevitably the slave of those more fortunate than himself.... deprivation of knowledge is a denial of the power to use liberty for great ends. An ignorant man may be free. . . . (But) he cannot employ his freedom so as to give him assurance of happiness."

Which of these conditions does Hinduism satisfy? How Hinduism is a denial of equality has already been made clear. It upholds privilege and inequality. Thus in Hinduism the very first condition for liberty is conspicuous by its absence.

Regarding economic security three things shine out in Hinduism. In the first place Hinduism denies freedom of a vocation. In the Scheme of Manu each man has his avocation preordained for him before he is born. Hinduism allows no choice. The occupation being preordained it has no relation to capacity nor to inclination.

In the second place Hinduism compels people to serve ends chosen by others. Manu tells the Shudra that he is born to serve the higher classes. He exhorts him to make that his ideal. Observe the following rules laid down by Manu.

> X. 121. If a Shudra (unable to subsist by serving Brahmanas) seeks a livelihood, he may serve Kshatriyas, or he may also seek to maintain himself by attending on a wealthy Vaishya.
>
> X. 122. But let a Shudra serve Brahmans....

Manu does not leave the matter of acting upto the ideal to the Shudra. He goes a step further and provides that the Shudra does not escape or avoid his destined task. For one of the duties enjoined by Manu upon the King is to see that all castes including the Shudra to discharge their appointed tasks.

> VIII. 410. "The king should order each man of the mercantile class to practice trade, or money lending, or agriculture and attendance on cattle; and each man of the servile class to act in the service of the twice born."
>
> VIII. 418. "With vigilant care should the king exert himself in compelling merchants and mechanics to perform their respective duties; for, when such men swerve from their duty, they throw this world into confusion."

Failure to maintain was made an offence in the King punishable at Law.

> VIII. 335. "Neither a father, nor a preceptor, nor a friend, nor a mother, nor a wife, nor a son, nor a domestic priest must be left

unpunished by the King, if they adhere not with firmness to their duty."

VIII. 336. "Where another man of lower birth would be fined one pana, the king shall be fined a thousand, and he shall give the fine to the priests, or cast it into the river, this is a sacred rule."

These rules have a two-fold significance, spiritual as well as economic. In the spiritual sense they constitute the gospel of slavery. This may not be quite apparent to those who know slavery only by its legal outward form and not by reference to its inner meaning. With reference to its inner meaning a slave as defined by Plato means a person who accepts from another the purposes which control his conduct. In this sense a slave is not an end in himself. He is only a means for filling the ends desired by others. Thus understood the Shudra is a slave. In their economic significance the Rules put an interdict on the economic independence of the Shudra. A Shudra, says Manu, must serve. There may not be much in that to complain of. The wrong however consists in that the rules require him to serve others. He is not to serve himself, which means that he must not strive after economic independence. He must forever remain economically dependent on others.

For as Manu says:—

I. 91. One occupation only the lord prescribed to the Shudra to serve meekly even these other three castes.

In the third place Hinduism leaves no scope for the Shudra to accumulate wealth. Manu's rules regarding the wages to be paid to the Shudra when employed by the three higher classes are very instructive on this point. Dealing with the question of wages to the Shudras, Manu says:—

X. 124. "They must allot to him (Shudra) out of their own family property a suitable maintenance, after considering his ability, his industry, and the number of those whom he is bound to support."

X. 125. "The remnants of their food must be given to him, as well as their old clothes, the refuse of their grain, and their old household furniture."

This is Manu's law of wages. It is not a minimum wage law. It is a maximum wage law. It was also an iron law fixed so low that there was no fear of the Shudra accumulating wealth and obtaining economic security. But Manu did not want to take chances and he went to the length of prohibiting the Shudra from accumulating property. He says imperatively:—

X. 129. No collection of wealth must be made by a Shudra even though he be able to do it; for a Shudra who has acquired wealth gives pain to Brahmans.

Thus in Hinduism, there is no choice of avocation. There is no economic independence and there is no economic security. Economically, speaking of a Shudra is a precarious thing.

In the matter of the spread of knowledge two conditions are prerequisites. There must be formal education. There must be literacy. Without these two, knowledge cannot spread. Without formal education it is not possible to transmit all the resources and achievements of a complex society. Without formal education the accumulated thought and experience relating to a subject cannot be made accessible to the young and which they will never get if they were left to pick up their training in informal association with others. Without formal education he will not get new perceptions. His horizon will not be widened and he will remain an ignorant slave of his routine work. But formal education involves the establishment of special agencies such as schools, books, planned materials such as studies etc. How can any one take advantage of these special agencies of formal education unless he is literate and able to read and write? The spread of the arts of reading and writing i.e. literacy and formal education go hand in hand. Without the existence of two there can be no spread of knowledge.

II. How does Hinduism stand in this matter?

The conception of formal education in Hinduism is of a very limited character. Formal education was confined only to the study of the Vedas. That was only natural. For the Hindus believed that there was no knowledge outside the Vedas. That being so formal education was confined to the study of the Vedas. Another consequence was that the Hindu recognized that its only duty was to study in the schools established for the study of the Vedas. These schools benefited only the Brahmins. The State did not hold itself responsible for opening establishments for the study of arts and sciences, which concerned the life of the merchant and the artisan. Neglected by the state they had to shift for themselves.

Each class managed to transmit to its members the ways of doing things it was traditionally engaged in doing. The duties of the Vaishya class required that a young Vaishya should know the rudiments of commercial geography, arithmetic, some languages as well as the practical details of trade. This he learned from his father in the course of the business. The Artisan's class or the Craftsman who sprang out of the `Shudra class also taught the arts and crafts to their children in the same way.' Education was domestic. Education was practical. It only increased the skill to do a *particular* thing. It did not lead to new perceptions. It did not widen horizon, with the result that the practical education taught him only an isolated and uniform way of acting so that in a changing environment the skill turned out to be gross ineptitude. Illiteracy became an inherent part of Hinduism by a process which is indirect but integral to Hinduism. To understand this process it is necessary to draw attention to rules framed by Manu in regard to the right to teach and study the Vedas. They are dealt with in the following Rules.

> I. 88. To the Brahmanas he (the creator) assigned *teaching* and *studying* the Veda.
>
> I. 89. The Kshatriya he (the creator) commanded to *study* the Veda.
>
> I. 90. The Vaishya he (the creator) commanded...... to study

the Veda.

II. 116. He who shall acquire knowledge of the Veda without the assent of his preceptor, incurs the guilt of stealing the scripture, and shall sink to the region of torment.

IV. 99. He (the twice born) must never read (the Veda)...... in the presence of the Shudras.

IX. 18. Women have no business with the text of the *Veda*.

XI. 199. A twice born man who has...... (improperly) divulged the Veda (i.e. to Shudras and women) (commits sin), atones for his offence, if he subsists a year on barley.

In these texts there are embodied three distinct propositions. The Brahmin, Kshatriya and Vaishya can study the Vedas. Of these the Brahmins alone have the right to teach the Vedas. But in the case of the Shudra he has not only not to study the Vedas but he should not be allowed to hear it read.

The successors of Manu made the disability of the Shudra in the matter of the study of the Veda into an offence involving dire penalties.

For instance Gautama says:—

XII. 4. If the Shudra intentionally listens for committing to memory the Veda, then his ears should be filled with (molten) lead and lac; if he utters the Veda, then his tongue should be cut off; if he has mastered the Veda his body should be cut to pieces.

To the same effect is Katyayana.

The ancient world may be said to have been guilty for failing to take the responsibility for the education of the masses. But never has any society been guilty of closing to the generality of its people the study of the books of its religion. Never has society been guilty of prohibiting the mass of its people from acquiring knowledge. Never has society made any attempt to declare that any attempt made by the common man to acquire knowledge shall be punishable as a crime. Manu is the only devine law giver who has denied the common man the right to knowledge.

But I cannot wait to dilate upon this. I am more immediately concerned in showing how the prohibition against the study of the Vedas to the mass of the people came to give rise to illiteracy and ignorance in secular life. The answer is easy. It must be realized that reading and writing have an integral connection with the teaching and study of the Vedas. Reading and writing were arts necessary for those who were free and privileged to study the Vedas. They were not necessary to those who were not free to do so. In this way reading and writing became incidental to the study of the Vedas. The result was that the theory of Manu regarding the rights and prohibitions in the matter of the teaching and the study of Vedas came to be extended to the arts of reading and writing. Those who had the right to study the Vedas were accorded the right to read and write. Those who had no right to study the Vedas were deprived of the right to read and write. So that it can be rightly said according to the law of Manu reading and writing has become the right of the high class few and illiteracy has become the destiny of the low class many.

Only a step in the process of this analysis will show how Manu by prohibiting literacy was responsible for the general ignorance in which the masses came to be enveloped.

Thus Hinduism far from encouraging spread of knowledge is a gospel of darkness.

Taking these facts into consideration Hinduism is opposed to the conditions in which liberty can thrive. It is therefore denial of liberty.

IV.

III. Does Hinduism recognize Fraternity?

There are two forces prevalent in Society. Individualism and Fraternity. Individualism is ever present. Every individual is ever asking "I and my neighbours, are we all brothers, are we even fiftieth cousins, am I their keeper, why should I do right to them" and under the pressure of his own particular interests acting as though he was an end to himself, thereby developing a non-social and even an anti-social self. Fraternity is a force of opposite character. Fraternity is another name for fellow feeling. It consists in a sentiment which leads an individual to identify himself with the good of others whereby "the good of others becomes to him a thing naturally and necessarily to be attended to like any of the physical conditions of our existence." It is because of this sentiment of fraternity that the individual does not "bring himself to think of the rest of his fellow-creatures as struggling rivals with him for the means of happiness, whom he must desire to see defeated in their object in order that he may succeed in his own." Individualism would produce anarchy. It is only fraternity, which prevents it and helps to sustain the moral order among men. Of this there can be no doubt.

How does this sentiment of Fraternity of fellow feeling arise? J. S. Mill says that this sentiment is a natural sentiment.

> "The social state is at once so natural, so necessary, and so habitual to man, that, except in some unusual circumstances or by an effort of voluntary abstraction he never conceives himself otherwise than as a member of a body; and this association is riveted more and more, as mankind are further removed from the state of savage independence. Any condition, therefore, which is essential to a state of society, becomes more and more an inseparable part of every person's conception of the state of things which he is born into, and which is the destiny of a human being. Now, society between human beings, except in the relation of master and slave, is manifestly impossible on any other footing than that the interests of all are to be consulted. Society between equals can only exist on the understanding that the interests of all are to be regarded equally. And since in all states of civilization, every per-

son, except an absolute monarch, has equals, every one is obliged to live on these terms with some body; and in every age some advance is made towards a state in which it will be impossible to live permanently on other terms with any body. In this way people grow up unable to conceive as possible to them a state of total disregard of other people's interests."

Does this sentiment of fellow feeling find a place among the Hindus? The following facts throw a flood of light on this question.

The first fact that strikes one is the number of castes. No body has made an exact computation of their number. But it is estimated that total is not less than 2000. It might be 3000. This is not the only distressing aspect of this fact. There are others. Castes are divided into sub-castes. Their number is legion. The total population of the Brahmin Caste is about a crore and a half. But there are 1886 sub-castes of the Brahmin Caste. In the Punjab alone the Saraswat Brahmins of the Province of Punjab are divided into 469 sub-castes. The Kayasthas of Punjab are divided into 590 sub-castes. One could go on giving figures to show this infinite process of splitting social life into small fragments.

The third aspect of this splitting process is the infinitely small fragments into which the Castes are split. Some of the Baniya sub-castes can count no more than 100 families. They are so inter related they find extremely difficult to marry within their castes without transgressing the rules of consanguinity.

It is noteworthy what small excuses suffice to bring about this splitting.

Equally noteworthy is the hierarchical character of the Caste System. Castes form an hierarchy in which one caste is at the top and is the highest, another at the bottom and it is the lowest and in between there are castes every one of which is at once above some castes and below some castes. The caste system is a system of gradation in which every caste except the highest and the lowest has a priority and precedence over some other castes.

How is this precedence or this superiority determined? This order of superiority and inferiority or this insubordination is determined by Rules (1) which are connected with religious rites and (2) which are connected with commensuality.

Religion as a basis of Rules of precedence manifests itself in three ways. Firstly through religious ceremonies, secondly through incantations that accompany the religious ceremonies and thirdly through the position of the priest.

Beginning with the ceremonies as a source of rules of precedence it should be noted that the Hindu Scriptures prescribe sixteen religious ceremonies. Although those are Hindu ceremonies every Hindu Caste cannot by right claim to perform all the sixteen ceremonies. Few can claim the right to perform all. Some are allowed to perform certain ceremonies, some are not allowed to perform certain of the ceremonies. For instance take the ceremony of Upanayan, wearing of the sacred thread. Some castes can't. Precedence follows this distinction in the matter of right to perform the ceremonies. A caste which can claim to perform all the ceremonies is higher in status than the caste which has a right to perform a few.

Turning to the Mantras, it is another source for rules of precedence. According to the Hindu Religion the same ceremony can be performed in two different ways. (1) Vedokta and (2) Puranokta. In the Vedokta form the ceremonies are performed with Mantras (incantations) from the Vedas. In the Puranokta form the ceremony is performed with Mantras (incantations) from the Puranas. Hindu Religious Scriptures fall into two distinct categories (1) The Vedas which are four, and (2) the Puranas which are eighteen. Although they are all respected as scriptures they do not all have the same sanctity. The Vedas have the highest sanctity and the Puranas have the lowest sanctity. The way the Mantras give rise to social precedence will be obvious if it is borne in mind that not every caste is entitled to have the ceremony performed in the Vedokta form. Three castes may well claim the right to the performance of one of the sixteen ceremonies. But it will be that one of it is entitled to perform it in the Vedokta form, another in the Puranokta form. Precedence goes with the kind of Mantra that a caste is entitled to use in the performance of a religious ceremony. A caste which is entitled to use Vedic Mantras is superior to a caste which is entitled to use only Puranokta Mantras.

Taking the priest as a second source of precedence connected with Religion, Hinduism requires the instrumentality of a priest for the derivation of the full benefit from the performance of a religious ceremony. The priest appointed by the scripture is the Brahmin. A Brahmin therefore is indispensable. But the scriptures do not require that a Brahmin shall accept the invitation of any and every Hindu irrespective of his caste to officiate at a religious ceremony. The invitation of which caste he will accept and of which he will refuse is a matter left to the wishes of the Brahmin. By long and well-established custom it is now settled at which caste he will officiate and at which caste he will not. This fact has become the basis of precedence as between castes. The caste at which a Brahmin will officiate is held as superior to a caste at whose religious functions a Brahmin will not officiate.

The second source for rules of precedence is commensality. It will be noticed that rules of marriage have not given rise to rules of precedence as rules of commensality have. The reason lies in the distinction between the rules prohibiting intermarriage and inter-dining. That difference is obvious. The prohibition on intermarriage is such that it cannot only be respected but it can be carried out quite strictly. But the prohibition of inter-dining creates difficulties. It cannot be carried out quite strictly in all places and under all circumstances. Man migrates and must migrate from place to place. In every place he happens to go he may not find his caste-men. He may find himself landed in the midst of strangers. Marriage is not a matter of urgency but food is. He can wait for getting himself married till he returns to the Society of his caste-men. But he cannot wait for his food. He must find it from somewhere and from someone. Question arises from which caste he can take food, if he has to. The rule is that he will take food from a caste above him but will not take food from a caste, which is below him. There is no way of finding how it came to be decided that a Hindu can take food from one caste and not from another. By long series of precedent every Hindu knows from what caste he can take food and from what caste he cannot. This is determined chiefly by the rule followed by the Brahmin. A caste is higher or lower according as the Brahmin takes from it food or not. In this connection the Brahmin has a very elaborate set of rules in the matter of food and water. (1) He will take only water from some and not from others. (2) A brahmin will not take food cooked in water by any caste. (3) He will take only food cooked in oil from some castes. Again he has a set of rules in the matter of the vessels, in which he will accept food and water. He will take food or water in an earthen vessel from some castes, only in metallic vessel from some and only in glass vessel from others. This goes to determine the level of the castes. If he takes food cooked in oil from a caste its status is higher than the caste from which he will not. If he takes water from a caste its status is higher than the caste from which he will not. If he takes water in a metallic vessel that caste is higher than the caste from which he will take water in an earthen vessel. Both these castes are higher than the caste from which he will take water in a glass vessel. Glass is a substance which is called (Nirlep) (which conserves no stain) therefore a Brahmin can take water in it even from the lowest. But other metals do conserve stains. Contaminating character of the stain depends upon the status of the person who has used it. That status depends upon the Brahmins will to accept water in that vessel.

These are some of the factors which determine the place and status of a caste in this Hindu hierarchical system of castes.

This hierarchical organization of the caste system is responsible for producing a social psychology, which is noteworthy. In the first place it produces a spirit of rivalry among the different castes for dignity. Secondly it produces an ascending scale of hatred and descending scale of contempt.

This social psychology of mutual hatred and contempt is well illustrated by the innumerable proverbs that are flying about in India. As examples I record a few of them.[21]

This spirit of hatred and contempt has not only found its place in proverbs but it has found its place in Hindu literature also. I refer to a Scripture known as the *Sahyadrikhand*. It is one of the Puranas which form a part of the Hindu Sacred literature. But its subject matter is totally foreign to the subject matter of other Puranas. It deals with the origin of the different castes. In doing so it assigns noble origin to other castes while it assigns to the Brahmin caste the filthiest origin. It was a revenge on Manu. It was worst lampoon on the Brahmins as a caste. The Peshwas very naturally ordered its destruction. Some survived the general destruction.

I will just record one more fact before I put the question.

Present day Hindus are probably the strongest opponents of Marxism. They are horrified at its doctrine of class struggle. But they forget that India has been not merely the land of class struggle but she has been the land of class wars.

The bitterest class war took place between the Brahmins and the Kshatriyas. The classical literature of the Hindus abounds in reference to class wars between these two Varnas.

> The first recorded conflict was between the Brahmins and King Vena. Vena was the son of King Anga, of the race of Atri

[21] *The proverbs are not mentioned in the MS*—Editors.

and was born of Sunitha, the daughter of Mrityu (Death). This son of the daughter of Kala (death), owing to the taint derived from his maternal grandfather, threw his duties behind his back, and lived in covetousness under the influence of desire. This king established an irreligious system of conduct; transgressing the ordinances of the Veda, he was devoted to lawlessness. In his reign men lived without study of the sacred books and the gods had no soma-libations to drink at sacrifices. `I' he declared, 'am the object, and the performer of sacrifice, and the sacrifice itself; it is to me that sacrifice should be presented, and oblation offered.' This transgressor of the rules of duty, who arrogated to himself what was not his due, was then addressed by all the great rishis, headed by Marichi. 'We are about to consecrate ourselves for a ceremony which shall last for many years, practice not unrighteousness, O Vena: this is not the eternal rule of duty. Thou art in every deed a Prajapati of Atri's race, and thou hast engaged to protect thy subjects.' The foolish Vena, ignorant of what was right, laughingly answered those great rishis who had so addressed him: 'Who but myself is the ordainer of duty or whom ought I to obey? Who on earth equals me in sacred knowledge, in prowess, in austere fervour, in truth? Ye who are deluded and senseless know not that I am the source of all beings and duties. Hesitate not to believe that I, if I willed, could burn up the earth, or deluge it with water, or close up heaven and earth.' When owing to his delusion and arrogance Vena could not be governed then the mighty rishis becoming incensed, seized the vigorous and struggling king, and rubbed his left thigh. From this thigh, so rubbed, was produced a black man, very short in stature, who, being alarmed, stood with joined hands. Seeing that he was agitated, Atri said to him 'Sit down' (Nishada). He became the founder of the race of the Nishadas, and also progenitor of the Dhivaras (fishermen), who sprang from the corruption of Vena. So two were produced from him the other inhabitants of the Vindhya range, the Tukharas and Tumburas, who are prone to lawlessness. Then the mighty sages, excited and incensed, again rubbed the right hand of Vena, as men do the Arani wood, and from it arose Pritha, respondent in body, glowing like the manifested Agni.

The son of Vena (Pritha) then, with joined hands, addressed the great Rishis: 'A very slender understanding for perceiving the principles of duty has been given to me by nature; tell me truly how I must employ it. Doubt not that I shall perform whatever thy shall declare to me as my duty, and its object.' Then those gods and great rishis said to him: 'Whatever duty is enjoined perform it without hesitation, disregarding what though mayest like or dislike, looking on all creatures with an equal eye, putting far from thee lust, anger, cupidity and pride. Restrain by the strength

> of thine arm all those men who swerve from righteousness, having a constant regard to duty. And in thought, act, and word take upon thyself, and continually renew, the engagement to protect the terrestrial Brahman (Veda or Brahmins?). . .. .. And promise that thou wilt exempt the Brahmans from punishment, and preserve society from the confusion of Castes.' The son of Vena then replied to the gods, headed by the rishis: 'The great Brahmans, the chief of men, shall be reverenced by me.' `So be it,' rejoined those declares of the Veda. Sukra, the depository of divine knowledge, became his Purohita; the Balakhilyas and Sarasvatyas his ministers; and the venerable Garga, the great rishi, his astrologer.
>
> The second recorded conflict took place between the Brahmins and the Kshatriya king Pururavas. A brief reference to it occurs in the Adiparva of the Mahabharat.
>
> Pururavas was born of lla. Ruling over thirteen islands of the ocean, and surrounded by beings who were all superhuman, himself a man of great renown, Pururavas, intoxicated by his prowess engaged in a conflict with the Brahmans, and robbed them of their jewels, although they loudly remonstrated. Sanatkumara came from Brahma's heaven, and addressed to him an admonition, which however, he did not regard. Being then straightway cursed by the incensed rishis, he perished, this covetous monarch, who, through pride of power, had lost his understanding. This glorious being (virat), accompanied Urvasi, brought down for the performance of sacred rites the fires which existed in the heaven of the Gandharvas, properly distributed into three.

A third collision is reported to have occurred between the Brahmins and King Nahusha. The story is given in great details in the Udyogaparva of the Mahabharat. It is there recorded:

> "After his slaughter of the demon Vrittra, Indra became alarmed at the idea of having taken the life of a Brahmin (for Vrittra was regarded as such), and hid himself in waters. In consequence of the disappearance of the king of gods, all affairs, celestial as well as terrestrial, fell into confusion. The rishis and Gods then applied to Nahusha to be their king. After at first excusing himself on the plea of want of power, Nahusha at length, in compliance with their solicitations, accepted the high function. Up to the period of his elevation he had led a virtuous life, but he now became addicted to amusement and sensual pleasure; and even aspired to the possession of Indrani, Indra's wife, whom he had happened to see. The queen resorted to the Angiras Vrihaspati, the preceptor of the Gods, who engaged to protect her. Nahusha was greatly incensed on hearing of this interference; but the Gods endeavoured to pacify him, and pointed out the immorality of appropriating another person's wife. Nahusha, however, would lis-

ten to no remonstrance, and insisted that in his adulterous designs he was not worse than Indra himself; "The renowned Ahalya, a rish's wife, was formerly corrupted by Indra in her husband's life-time; why was he not prevented by you? And many barbarous acts, and unrighteous deeds, and frauds were perpetrated of by old Indra; Why was he not prevented by you?" The Gods, urged by Nahusha, then went to bring Indrani; but Vrihaspati would not give her up. At his recommendation, however, she solicited Nahusha for some delay, till she should ascertain what had become of her husband. This request was granted. The Gods next applied to Vishnu on behalf of Indra; and Vishnu promised that if Indra would sacrifice to him, he should be purged from his guilt, and recover his dominion, while Nahusha would be destroyed. Indra sacrificed accordingly; and the result is thus told; "Having divided the guilt of Brahmanicide among trees, rivers, mountains, the earth, women and the elements, Vasava (Indra), lord of the Gods, became freed from suffering and sin, and self governed." Nahusha was by this means, shaken from his place. But he must have speedily regained his position, as we are told that Indra was again ruined, and became invisible. Indrani now went in search of her husband; and by the help of Upasriti (the Goddess of night and revealer of secrets) discovered him existing in a very subtle form in the stem of a lotus growing in a lake situated in a continent within an ocean north of the Himalaya. She made known to him the wicked intention of Nahusha, and entreated him to exert his power, rescue her from danger, and resume his dominion. Indra declined any immediate interposition on the plea of Nahusha's superior strength; but suggested to his wife a device by which the usurper might be hurled from his position. She was recommended to say to Nahusha that "if he would visit her on a celestial vehicle borne by rishis, she would with pleasure submit herself to him." The question of the Gods accordingly went to Nahusha, by whom she was graciously received, and made this proposal: "I desire for thee, king of the Gods, a vehicle hitherto unknown, such as neither Vishnu, nor Rudra, nor the asuras, nor the rakshases employ. Let the eminent rishis, all united, bear thee, lord, in a car; this idea pleases me." Nahusha receives favourably this appeal to his vanity, and in the course of his reply thus gives utterance to his self congratulation: "He is a personage of no mean prowess who makes the *Munis* his bearers. I am a fervid devotee of great might, lord of the past, the future and the present. If I were angry the world would no longer stand; on me everything depends.... Wherefore, O Goddess I shall, without doubt, carry out what you propose. The seven rishis, and all the Brahman rishis, shall carry me. Behold beautiful Goddess, my majesty and my prosperity." The narrative goes on: "Accordingly this wicked being, irreligious, violent, intoxicated by the force of conceit, and arbitrary in his conduct, attached to his car the rishis, who submitted to his commands, and compelled them to bear him." Indrani then again resorts to Vrihaspati, who assures her that vengeance will soon overtake Nahusha for his presumption; and promises that he will himself perform a sacrifice with a view to the destruction of the oppressor, and the discovery of Indra's lurking place. Agni is then sent to discover and bring Indra to Vrihaspati; and the latter, on Indra's arrival, informs him of all that had occurred during his absence. While Indra with Kuvera, Yama, Soma, and Varuna, was devising means for the destruction of Nahusha, the sage Agastya came up, congratulated Indra on the fall of his rival, and proceeded to relate how it had occurred: Wearied with carrying the sinner Nahusha, the eminent divine rishis, and the spotless brahman-rishis asked that divine personage Nahusha (to solve) a difficulty: 'Dost thou, Vasava, most excellent of conquerors, regard as authoritative or not those Brahmana texts which are recited at the immolation of king?' 'No', replied Nahusha, whose understanding was enveloped in darkness. The rishis rejoined: 'Engaged in unrighteousness, thou attainest not unto righteousness: these texts, which were formerly uttered by great rishis, are regarded by us as authoritative.' The (proceeds Agastya) disputing with the munis, impelled by unrighteousness, touched me on the head with his foot. In consequence of this the king's glory was smitten and his prosperity departed. When he had instantly become agitated and oppressed with fear, I said to him, 'Since thou, O fool, condemnest that sacred text, always held in honour, which has been composed by former sages, and employed by Brahman-rishis, and hast touched my head with thy foot, and employest the Brahma—like and irresistable rishis as bearers to carry thee,—therefore, short of thy lustre and all thy merit exhausted, sink down, sinner, degraded from heaven to earth. For then thousand years thou shalt crawl in the form of a huge serpent. When that period is completed, thou shalt again ascend to heaven.' So fell that wicked wretch from the sovereignty of the Gods."

Next there is a reference to the conflict between King Nimi and the Brahmins. The Vishnu Puran relates the story as follows:—

"Nimi had requested the Brahman-rishi Vasishtha to officiate at a sacrifice, which was to last a thousand years, Vasishtha in reply pleaded a pre-engagement to Indra for five hundred years, but promised to return at the end of that period. The king made no remark, and Vasishtha went away, supposing that he had assented to this arrangement. On his return, however, the priest discovered that Nimi had retained Gautama (who was equal with Vasishtha a Brahman-rishi) and others to perform the sacrifices;

> and being incensed at the neglect to give him notice of what was intended, he cursed the king, who was then asleep, to lose his corporeal form. When Nimi awoke and learnt that he had been cursed without any previous warning, he retorted, by uttering a similar curse on Vasishtha, and then died. In consequence of this curse the vigour of Vasistha, however, received from them another body when their seed had fallen from them at the sight of Urvasi. Nimi's body was embalmed. At the close of the sacrifice which he had begun, the Gods were willing, on the intercession of the priests, to restore him to life, but he declined the offer, and was placed by the deities, according to his desire, in the eyes of all living creatures. It is in consequence of this fact that they are always opening the shutting (nimishas means "the twinkling of the eye")."

Manu mentions another conflict between the Brahmins and King Sumukha. But of this no details are available.

These are instances of conflict between the Brahmins and the Kshatriya Kings. From this it must not be supposed that the Brahmins and the Kshatriyas as two classes did not clash. That there were clashes between these two classes as distinguished from conflicts with kings is abundantly proved by material the historic value of which cannot be doubted. Reference may be made to three events.

First is the contest between two individuals Vishvamitra the Kshatriya and Vasishtha the Brahmin. The issue between the two was whether a Kshatriya can claim Brahmahood. The story is told in Ramayana and is as follows:—

> There was formerly, we are told, a king called Kusa, son of Prajapati, who had a son called Kushanabha, who was father of Gadhi, the father of Visvamitra. The latter ruled the earth for many thousand years. On one occasion, when he was making a circuit of the earth, he came to Vasishtha's hermitage, the pleasant abode of many saints, sages, and holy devotees, where, after at first declining he allowed himself to be hospitably entertained with his followers. Visvamitra, however, coveting the wondrous cow, which had supplied all the dainties of the feast, first of all asked that she should be given to him in exchange for a hundred thousand common cows, adding that "she was a gem, that gems were the property of the king, and that, therefore, the cow was his by right." On this price being refused the king advances immensely in his offers, but all without effect. He then proceeds—very ungratefully and tyrannically, it must be allowed—to have the cow removed by force, but she breaks away from his attendants, and rushes back to her master, complaining that he was deserting her. He replied that he was not deserting her, but that the king was much more powerful than he. She answers, "Men do not ascribe strength to a Kshatriya; the Brahmins are stronger. The Strength of Brahmins is divine, and superior to that of Ksha-

triya. Thy strength is immeasurable. Visvamitra, though of great vigour, is not more powerful than thou. Thy energy is invincible. Commission me, who have been acquired by the Brahmanical power, and I will destroy the pride, and force, and attempt of this wicked prince." She accordingly by her bellowing creates hundreds of Pahlavas, who destroy the entire host of Visvamitra, but are slain by him in their turn. Sakas and Yavans, of great power and valour, and well armed, were then produced who consumed the king's soldiers, but were routed by him. The cow then calls into existence by her bellowing, and from different parts of her body, other warriors of various tribes, who again destroyed Visvamitra's entire army, foot soldiers, elephants, horses, chariots, and all. A hundred of the monarch's sons, armed with various weapons, then rushed in great fury on Vashistha, but were all reduced to ashes in a moment by the blast of that sage's mouth. Vishvamitra, being thus utterly vanquished and humbled, appointed one of his sons to be regent, and travelled to the Himalaya, where he betook himself to austerities, and thereby obtained a vision of Mahadeva, who at his desire revealed to him the science of arms in all its branches, and gave him celestial weapons with which, elated and full of pride, he consumed the hermitage of Vashishtha, and put its inhabitants to flight. Vashishtha then threatens Vishvamitra and uplifts his Brahminical mace. Vishvamitra too, raises his fiery weapon and calls out to his adversary to stand. Vashishtha bids him to show his strength, and boasts that he will soon humble his pride. He asks: "What comparison is there between a Kshatriya's might, and the great might of a Brahman? Behold, thou contemptible Kshatriya, my divine Brahmanical power." The dreadful fiery weapon uplifted by the son of Gadhi was then quenched by the rod of the Brahman, as fire is by water. Many and various other celestial missiles, as the nooses of Brahma, Kala (time), and Varuna, the discus of Vishnu, and the trident Siva, were hurled by Vishvamitra at his antagonist, but the son of Brahma swallowed them up in his all-devouring mace. Finally, to the intense consternation of all the Gods, the warrior shot off the terrific weapon of Brahma (Brahmastra); but this was equally ineffectual against the Brahmanical sage. Vashishtha had now assumed a direful appearance: "Jets of fire mingled with smoke darted from the pores of his body; the Brahminical mace blazed in his hand like a smokeless mundane conflagration, or a second sceptre of Yama." Being appeased, however, by the munis, who proclaimed his superiority to his rival, the sage stayed his vengeance; and Vishvamitra exclaimed with a groan: 'Shame on a Kshatriya's strength; the strength of a Brahman's might alone is strength; by the single Brahmanical mace all my weapons have been destroyed.' No alternative now remains, to the humiliated monarch, but either to acquiesce in this helpless inferiority, or to work out his own elevation to the Brahmanical order. He embraces the latter alternative: "Having pondered well this defeat, I shall betake myself, with composed senses and mind, to strenous austere fervour, which shall exalt me to the rank of a Brahman." Intensely vexed and mortified, groaning and full of hatred against his enemy, he travelled with his queen to the south, and carried his resolution into effect; and we are first of all told that three sons Havishyanda, Madhusyanda, and Dridhanetra were born to him. At the end of a thousand years Brahma appeared, and announced that he had conquered the heaven of royal sages (Rajarshis); and, in consequence of his austere fervour, he was recognised as having attained that rank. Vishvamitra, however, was ashamed, grieved, and incensed at the offer of so very inadequate a reward, and exclaimed: "I have practised intense austerity, and the Gods and Rishis regard me only as a Rajarshi and not as a Brahman." There is conflict recorded between the same persons or different persons of the same name though on a somewhat different issue.

King Trisanku, one of Ikshvaku's descendants, had conceived the design of celebrating a sacrifice by virtue of which he should ascent bodily to heaven. As Vashistha, on being summoned, declared that the thing was impossible (asakyam), Trisanku travelled to the south, where the sage's hundred sons were engaged in austerities, and applied to them to do what their father had declined. Though he addressed them with the greatest reverence and humility, and added that "the Ikshvaku regarded their family—priests as their highest resource in difficulties, and that, after their father, he himself looked to them as his tutelary deities" he received from the haughty priests the following rebuke for his presumption: "Asakyam" "Fool, thou hast been refused by thy truth speaking preceptor. How is it that, disregarding his authority, thou hast resorted to another school (sakha). The family priest is the highest oracle of all the Ikshvakus; and the command of that veracious personages cannot be transgressed. Vashishtha, the divine Rishi, has declared that 'the thing cannot be'; and how can we undertake thy sacrifice? Thou art foolish king; return to thy capital. The divine (Vashishtha) is competent to act as priest of the three worlds; how can we shew him disrespect?" Trisanku then gave them to understand that as his preceptor and "his preceptor's sons had declined compliance with his requests, he should think of some other expedient." In consequence of his venturing to express this presumptuous intention, they condemned him by their imprecation to become a Chandala. As this curse soon took effect, and the unhappy king's form was changed into that of a degraded outcast, he resorted to Vishvamitra (who, as we have seen, was also dwelling at this period in the south), enlarging on his own virtues and piety, and bewailing his fate. Vishvamitra commiserated his condition, and promised to sacrifice on his behalf, and exalt him to heaven in the same Chandala form to which he had been condemned by his preceptor's curse. "Heaven is now as good as in thy possession, since thou hast resorted to the son of Kusika." He then directed that preparations should be made for the sacrifice, and that all the Rishis, including the family of Vashishtha should be invited to the ceremony. The disciples of Vishvamitra, who had conveyed his message, reported the result on their return in these words: "Having heard your message, all the Brahmans are assembling in all the countries, and have arrived, excepting Mahodaya (Vashishtha)?" Hear what dreadful words those hundred Vashishthas, their voices quivering with rage, have uttered: "How can the Gods and Rishis consume the oblation at the sacrifice of that man, especially if he be a Chandala, for whom a Kshatriya is officiating priest? How can illustrious Brahmans ascend to heaven after eating the food of a Chandala, and being entertained by Vishvamitra?" These ruthless words all Vashishthas, together with Mahodaya, uttered, their eyes inflamed with anger. Vishvamitra, who was greatly incensed on receiving this, message by a curse doomed the sons of Vashishtha to be reduced to ashes, and reborn as degraded outcasts (mritapah) for seven hundred births, and Mahodaya to become a Nishada. Knowing that this curse had taken effect, Vishvamitra then after eulogizing Trisanku, proposed to the assembled Rishis that the sacrifice should be celebrated. To this they assented, being actuated by fear of the terrible sage's wrath. Vishvamitra himself officiated at the sacrifices as yajakas; and the other Rishis as priests (Ritvijah) (with other functions) performed all the ceremonies. Vishvamitra next invited the gods to partake of the oblations; "When, however, the deities did not come to receive their portions, Vishvamitra became full of wrath, and raising aloft the sacrificial ladle, thus addressed Trisanku: 'Behold, O monarch, the power of austere fervour acquired by my own efforts. I myself, by my own energy, will conduct thee to heaven. Ascend to that celestial region which is so arduous to attain in an earthly body. I have surely earned SOME reward of my austerity." Trisanku ascended instantly to heaven in the sight of Munis. Indra, however, ordered him to be gone, as a person who, having incurred the curse of his spiritual preceptors, was unfit for the abode of the celestials:—and to fall down headlong to earth. He accordingly began to descend, invoking loudly, as he fell, the help of his spiritual patron. Vishvamitra, greatly incensed, called out to him to stop: "Then by the power of his divine knowledge and austere fervour created, like another Prajapati, other Seven Rishis (a constellation so called) in the southern part of the sky. Having proceeded to this quarter of the heavens, the renowned sage, in the midst of the Rishis, formed another garland of stars, being overcome with fury. Exclaiming, 'I will create another Indra, or the world shall have no Indra at all', he began, in his rage, to call Gods also into being." The Rishis, Gods, (Suras), and Asuras now became seriously alarmed and said to Vishvamitra, in a concilliatory tone, that Trisanku, "as he had been cursed by his preceptors, should not be admitted bodily into heaven, until he had undergone some lustration." The sage replied that he had given a promise to Trisanku, and appealed to the Gods to permit his portage to remain bodily in heaven, and the newly created stars to retain their places in perpetuity. The Gods agreed that "these numerous stars should remain, but beyond the Sun's path, and that Trisanku, like an immortal, with his head downwards should shine among them, and be followed by them," adding "that his object would be thus attained, and his renown secured, and he would be like a dweller in heaven." Thus was this great dispute adjusted by a compromise, which Vishvamitra accepted.[22]

When all the Gods and rishis had departed at the conclusion of the sacrifice, Vishvamitra said to his attendant devotees: "This has been a great interruption (to our austerities) which has occurred in the southern region; we must proceed in another direction to continue our penances." He accordingly went to a forest in the west, and began his austerities anew. Here the narrative is again interrupted by the introduction of another story, that of king Ambarisha, king of Ayodhya, who was, according to the Ramayana, the twenty eighth in descent from Ikshvaku, and the twenty second from Trisanku. Vishvamitra is nevertheless represented as flourishing contemporaneously with both of these princes. The story relates that Ambarisha was engaged in performing a sacrifice, when Indra carried away the victim. The priest said that this ill-omened event had occurred owing to the king's bad administration; and would call for a great expiation, unless a human victim could be produced. After a long search the royal rishi (Ambarisha) came upon the Brahmin-rishi Richika, a descendant of Bhrigu, and asked him to sell one of his sons for a victim, at the price of a hundred thousand cows. Richika answered that he would not sell his eldest son; and his wife added that she would not sell the youngest: "Eldest sons," she observed, "being generally the favourites of their fathers, and youngest sons of their mothers." The second son, Sunassepa then said that in that case he regarded himself as the one who was to be sold, and desired the king to remove him. The hundred thousand cows,

[22] This is the story of Trisanku. It will have been observed, it differs materially from the one quoted above from Harivansa; but brings out more distinctly the character of the conflict between Vashishtha and Vishvamitra.

with ten millions of gold pieces and heaps of jewels, were paid down, and Sunassepa was carried away. As they were passing through Puskara, Sunassepa beheld his maternal uncle Vishvamitra who was engaged in austerities there with other rishis, threw himself into his arms, and implored his assistance, urging his orphan, friendless, and helpless state, as claims on the sage's benevolence. Vishvamitra soothed him; and pressed his own sons to offer themselves as victims in the room of Sunassepa. This proposition met with no favour from Madhushanda and the other sons of the royal hermit, who answered with haughtiness and derison: "How is it that thou sacrificest thine own sons, and seekest to rescue those of others? We look upon this as wrong, and like the eating of one's own flesh." The sage was exceedingly wrath at this disregard of his injunction, and doomed his sons to be born in the most degraded classes, like Vashishtha's sons, and to eat dog's flesh, for a thousand years. He then said to Sunassepa: "When thou art bound with hallowed cords, decked with a red garland, and anointed with unguents, and fastened to the sacrificial post of Vishnu, then address thyself to Agni, and sing these two divine verses (gathas), at the sacrifice of Ambarisha; then shall thou attain the fulfilment of thy desire." Being furnished with the two gathas, Sunassepa proposed at once to King Ambarisha that they should set out for their destination. Then bound at the stake to be immolated, dressed in a red garment, "he celebrated the two Gods, Indra and his younger brother (Vishnu), with the excellent verses. The thousand-eyed (Indra) was pleased with the sacred hymn, and bestowed long life on Sunassepa." King Ambarisha also received great benefits from this sacrifice. Vishvamitra meanwhile proceeded with his austerities, which he prolonged for a thousand years. "At the end of this time the Gods came to allot his reward; and Brahma announced that he had attained the rank of a rishi, thus apparently advancing an additional step." Dissatisfied, as it would seem, with this, the sage commenced his task of penance anew. After a length of time he beheld the nymph (Apsara) Menka, who had come to bathe in the lake of Pushkara. She flashed on his view, unequalled in her radiant beauty, like lightning in a cloud. He was smitten by her charms, invited her to be his companion in his hermitage, and for ten years remained a slave to her witchery, to the great prejudice of his austerities. At length he became ashamed of this ignoble subjection, and full of indignation at what he believed to be a device of the Gods to disturb his devotion; and, dismissing the nymph with gentle accents, he departed for the northern mountains, where he practised severe austerities for a thousand years on the banks of the Kausiki river. The Gods became alarmed at the progress he was making, and decided that he should be dignified with the appellation of great rishi (Maharshi); and Brahma, giving effect to the general opinion of the deities, announced that he had conferred that rank upon him. Joining his hands and bowing his head, Vishvamitra replied that he should consider himself to have indeed completely subdued his senses, if the incomparable title of Brahmin-rishi were conferred upon him. Brahma informed him in answer, that he had not yet acquired the power of perfectly controlling his senses; but should make further efforts with that view. The sage then began to put himself through a yet more rigorous course of austerities, standing with his arms erect, without support, feeding on air, in summer exposed to five fires (i.e. one on each of four sides, and the sun overhead), in the rainy season remaining unsheltered from the wet, and in winter lying on a watery couch night and day. This he continued for a thousand years. At last Indra and the other deities became greatly distressed at the idea of the merit he was storing up, and the power which he was thereby acquiring; and the chief of the celestials desired the nymph Rambha to go and bewitch him by her blandishments. She expressed great reluctance to expose herself to the wrath of the formidable muni, but obeyed the repeated injunction of Indra, who promised that he and Kandarpa (the God of love) should stand by her, and assumed her most attractive aspect with the view of overcoming the sage's impassability. He, however, suspected this design, and becoming greatly incensed, he doomed the nymph by a curse to be turned into stone and to continue in that state for a thousand years. The curse took effect, and Kandarpa and Indra sunk away. In this way, though he resisted the allurements of sensual love, he lost the whole fruit of his austerities by yielding to anger; and had to begin his work over again. He resolved to check his irresistibility, to remain silent, not even to breathe for hundreds of years; to dry up his body; and to fast and stop his breath till he had obtained the coveted character of a Brahmin. He then left the Himalaya and travelled to the east, where he underwent a dreadful exercise, unequalled in the whole history of austerities, maintaining silence, according to a vow, for a thousand years. At the end of this time he had attained to perfection, and although thwarted by many obstacles, he remained unmoved by anger. On the expiration of this course of austerity, he prepared some food to eat; which Indra, coming in the form of a Brahmin, begged that he would give him. Vishvamitra did so, and though he had done left for himself, and was obliged to remain fasting, he said nothing to the Brahmin, on account of his vow of silence. "As he continued to suspend his breath, smoke issued from his head, to the great consternation and distress of the three worlds." The Gods, rishis, etc., then addressed Brahma. "The great muni Vishvamitra has been allured and provoked in various ways, but still advances in his

> sanctity. If his wish is not conceded, he will destroy the three worlds by the force of his austerity. All the regions of the universe are confounded, no light anywhere shines; all the oceans are tossed, and the mountains crumble, the earth quakes, and the wind blows confusedly. We cannot, O Brahma, guarantee that mankind shall not become atheistic..... Before the great and glorious sage of fiery form resolves to destroy (everything) let him be propitiated." The Gods, headed by Brahma, then addressed Vishvamitra: 'Hail, Brahman rishi, we are gratified by the austerity; O Kausika, thou hast, through their intensity, attained to Brahmahood. O Brahman, associated with the Maruts, confers on thee long life. May every blessing attend thee; depart where ever thou wilt.' The sage, delighted, made his obeisance to the Gods, and said: 'If I have obtained Brahmahood, and long life, then let the mystic monosyllable (omkara) and the sacrificial formula (vashatkara) and the Vedas recognise me in that capacity. And let Vashishtha, the son of Brahmin, the most eminent of those who are skilled in the Kshatra-Veda, and the Brahma-Veda (the knowledge of the Kshatriya and the Brahmnical disciplines), address me similarly' ..... Accordingly Vashishtha, being propitiated by the Gods, became reconciled to Vishvamitra, and recognised his claim to all the prerogatives of a Brahman rishi. .... Vishvamitra, too having attained the Brahmanical rank, paid all honour to Vashishtha.

The second event has a reference to the slaughter of the Brahmins by the Kshatriyas. It is related in the Adiparva of the Mahabharat from which the following account is taken:—

> "There was a King named Kritrvirya, by whose liberality the Bhrigus, learned in the Vedas, who officiated as his priests, had been greatly enriched with corn and money. After he had gone to heaven, his descendants were in want of money, and came to beg for a supply from the Bhrigus, of whose wealth they were aware. Some of the latter hid their money under ground, others bestowed it on Brahmins, being afraid of the Kshatriyas, while others again gave these last what they wanted. It happened, however, that a Kshatriya, while digging the ground, discovered some money buried in the house of Bhrigu. The Kshatriyas then assembled and saw this treasure, and, being incensed, slew in consequence all the Bhrigus, who they regarded with contempt, down to the children in the womb. The widows, however, fled to the Himalaya mountains. One of them concealed her unborn child in her thigh. The Kshatriya, hearing of its existence from a Brahmani informant, sought to kill it; but it issued forth from its mother's thigh with lustre, and blinded the persecutors. After wandering about bewildered among the mountains for a time, they humbly supplicated the mother of the child for the restoration of their

> sight; but she referred them to her wonderful infant Aurva into whom the whole Veda, with its six Vedangas, had entered as the person who (in retaliation of the slaughter of his relatives) had robbed them of their eyesight, and who alone could restore it. They accordingly had recourse to him, and their eyesight was restored. Aurva, however, meditated the destruction of all living creatures, in revenge for the slaughter of the Bhrigus, and entered on a course of austerities which alarmed both Gods, Asuras, and men; but his progenitors (Pitris) themselves appeared, and sought to turn him from his purpose by saying that they had no desire to be revenged on the Kshatriyas: "It was not from weakness that the devout Bhrigus overlooked the massacre perpetrated by the murderous Kshatriyas. When we became distressed by old age, we ourselves desired to be slaughtered by them. The money which was buried by someone in a Bhrigu's house was placed there for the purpose of exciting hatred, by those who wished to provoke the Kshatriyas. For what had we, who were desiring heaven, to do with money?" They added that they hit upon this device because they did not wish to be guilty of suicide, and concluded by calling upon Aurva to restrain his wrath; and abstain from the sin he was meditating, "Destroy not the Kshatriyas. Oh, son, nor the seven worlds. Suppress thy kindled anger which nullifies the power of austere fervour." Aurva, however, replies that he cannot allow his threat to remain un-executed. His anger, unless wreaked upon some other object, will, he says, consume himself. And he argues on grounds of justice, expediency, and duty, against the clemency which his progenitors recommend. He is, however, persuaded by the Pitris to throw the fire of his anger into the sea, where they say it will find exercise in assailing the watery element, and in this way his threat will be fulfilled."

The third event has reference to the slaughter of the Kshatriyas by the Brahmins. This story is told in several places in the Mahabharat.

> The magnificent and mighty Kartavirya, possessing a thousand arms, was lord of this whole world, living in Mahishmati. This Haihaya of unquestioned valour ruled over the whole sea-girt earth, with its oceans and continents. He obtained boons from the Muni Dattatreya, a thousand arms whenever he should go into battle, power to make the conquest of the whole earth, a disposition to rule it with justice and the promise of instruction from the virtuous in the event of his going astray. Then ascending his chariot glorious as the resplendent Sun, he exclaimed in the intoxication of his prowess, 'Who is like me in fortitude, courage, fame, heroism, energy, and vigour?' At the end of this speech a bodiless voice in the sky addressed him: 'Thou knowest not, O fool, that a Brahman is better than Kshatriya. It is with the help

> of the Brahman that the Kshatriya rules his subjects.' Arjuna answers: 'If I am pleased, I can create, or, if displeased, annihilate living beings; and no Brahman is superior to me in act, thought or word. The first proposition is that the Brahmins are superior; the second that the Kshatriyas are superior; both of these thou hast stated with their grounds, but there is a difference between them (in point of force). The Brahmins are dependent on the Kshatriyas and not the Kshatriyas on the Brahmins, who wait upon them, and only make the Vedas a pretence. Justice, the protection of the people, has its seat in the Kshatriyas. From them the Brahmins derive their livelihood; how then can the latter be superior? I always keep in subjection myself those Brahmins, the chief of all beings, who subsist on air and sand who have a high opinion of themselves. For truth was spoken by that female the Gayatri in the sky. I shall subdue all those unruly Brahmins clad in hides. No one in the three worlds, god or man can hurl me from my royal authority; therefore I am superior to any Brahman. Now shall I turn the world in which Brahmins have the upper hand into a place where Kshatriyas shall have the upper hand; for no one dares to encounter my force in battle.' Hearing this speech of Arjun, the female roving in the night became alarmed. Then Vayu hovering in the air, said to Arjuna: 'Abandon this sinful disposition, and do obeisance to the Brahmins. If thou shall do them wrong, thy kingdom shall be convulsed. They will subdue thee; those powerful men will humble thee, and expel thee from thy country.' The King asks him, 'Who art thou?' Vayu replies, 'I am Vayu, the messenger of the Gods and tell thee what is for thy benefit.' Arjuna rejoins, 'Oh, thou displayest today a great warmth of devotion to the Brahmins. But say that a Brahman is like (any other) earthhorn creature.'

This king came into conflict with Parsuram the son of a Brahman sage Jamadagni. The history of this conflict is as follows:—

> There lived a king of Kanyakubja, called Gadhi, who had a daughter named Satyavati. The marriage of this princess to the rishi Richika, and the birth of Jamadagni, are then told in nearly the same way as above narrated. Jamadagni and Satyavati had five sons, the youngest of whom was the redoubtable Parasuram. By his father's command he kills his mother (who, by the indulgence of impure desire, had fallen from her previous sanctity), after the four elder sons had refused this matricidal offence, and had in consequence been deprived of reason by their father's curse. At Parasuram's desire, however, his mother is restored by his father to life, and his brothers to reason; and he himself is absolved from all the guilt of murder; and obtains the boon of invincibility and long life from his father. His history now begins to be connected

> with that of king Arjuna (or Kartavirya). The latter had come to Jamadagni's hermitage, and had been respectfully received by his wife; but he had requited this honour by carrying away by force the calf of the sage's sacrificial cow, and breaking down his lofty trees. On being informed of this violence, Parasurama was filled with indignation, attacked Arjuna, cut off his thousand arms, and slew him. Arjuna's sons, in return slew the peaceful sage Jamadagni, in the absence of Parasuram.
>
> Rama, after performing, on his return, his father's funeral obsequies, vowed to destroy the whole Kshatriya race; and executed his threat by killing first Arjun's sons and their followers. Twenty one times did he sweep away all the Kshatriyas from the earth, and formed five lakes of blood in Samantpanchaka; in which he satiated the manes of the Bhrigus, and beheld face to face (his grandfather), Richika, who addressed himself to Rama. The latter gratified Indra by offering to him a grand sacrifice, and gave the earth to the officiating priests. He bestowed also a golden altar, ten fathoms long and nine high, on the mighty Kasyapa. This, by his permission, the Brahmins divided among themselves, deriving thence the name of Khandavavanas. Having given away the earth to Kasyapa, Parasuram himself dwells on the mountain Mahendra. Thus did enmity arise between him and Kshatriyas, and thus was the earth conquered by Parasuram of boundless might.

The Kshatriyas who were slain by Parasuram are described in the Dronaparvan of the Mahabharata as of various provinces, viz., Kasmiras, Daradas, Kuntis, Kshudrakas, Malavas, Angas, Vangas, Kalingas, Videhas, Tamraliptakas, Marttikavatas, Sivis and other Rajanyas.

The means by which the Kshattriya race was restored is also told as part of this story of annihilation of the Kshatriyas by the Brahmins. It is said:—

> "Having one and twenty times swept away all the Kshatriyas from the earth, the son of Jamdagni engaged in austerities on Mahendra the most excellent of mountains. After he had cleared the world of Kshatriyas, their widows came to the Brahmins, praying for offspring. The religious Brahmins, free from any impulse of lust cohabited at the proper seasons with these women, who in consequence became pregnant, and brought forth valiant Kshatriya boys and girls, to continue the Kshatriya stock. Thus was the Kshatriya race virtuously begotten by Brahmins on Kshatriya women, and became multiplied and long lived. Thence there arose four castes inferior to the Brahmins."

No country has such a dismal record of class war as Hindustan. It was the proud boast of the Brahmin Parsuram that he exterminated the Kshatriyas twenty one times from the face of Hindustan and recreated them by Brahmans cohabiting with the widows of the Kshatriyas.

It must not be supposed that this Class War in India is a matter of ancient History. It has been present all along. Its existence was very much noticeable in Maharashtra during the Maratha Rule. It destroyed the Maratha Empire. It must not be supposed that these class Wars were like ordinary wars which are a momentary phenomena which come and go and which leave no permanent chasms to divide the peoples of the different nations. In India the class war is a permanent phenomenon, which is silently but surely working its way. It is a grain in the life and it has become genius of the Hindus.

These facts it will not be denied are symptomatic in the sense they indicate health and character. Do they suggest that there is fraternity among Hindus? In the face of these facts I am sure it would be impossible to give an affirmative answer.

What is the explanation of this absence of fraternity among the Hindus? It is Hinduism and its philosophy that is responsible for it. The sentiment of fraternity as Mill said is natural but it is a plant, which grows only where the soil is propitious and the conditions for its growth exist. The fundamental condition for the growth of the sentiment of fraternity is not preaching that we are children of God or the realization that one's life is dependent upon others. It is too rational to give rise to a sentiment. The condition for the growth of this sentiment of fraternity lies in sharing in the vital processes of life. It is sharing in the joys and sorrows of birth, death, marriage and food. Those who participate in these come to feel as brothers. Prof. Smith very rightly emphasizes the importance of sharing food as a prime factor in the creation of community feeling when he says;

> "The sacrificial meal was an appropriate expression of the antique ideal of religious life, not merely because it was a social act and in which the God and his worshippers were conceived as partaking together, but because, as has already been said, the very act of eating and drinking with a man was a symbol and a confirmation of fellowship and mutual social obligations. The one thing directly expressed in the sacrificial meal is that the God and his worshippers are commensals but every other point in their mutual relations is included in what this involves. Those who sit at meal together are united for all social effects; those who do not eat together are aliens to one another, without fellowship in religion and without reciprocal social duties."[23]

There is no sharing among Hindus of joys and sorrows involved in the vital facts of life. Everything is separate and exclusive. The Hindu is separate and exclusive all through his life. A foreigner coming to India will not find men crying Hindu Pani (water for Hindus) and Musalman Pani (water for Musalmans). He will find Brahmin Coffee Houses, Brahmin Eating-Houses, where no non-Brahmin Hindus can go. He will find Brahmin Maternity Homes, Maratha Maternity Homes and Bhatia Maternity Homes although Brahmins, Marathas and Bhatias

[23] The Religion of the Semites—p. 269.

are all Hindus. If there is a birth at the house of a Brahmin, no non-Brahmin will be invited nor will he feel the desire to join. If there is marriage in the family of a Brahmin, no non-Brahmin will be invited nor will he feel the desire to join if a Brahmin dies, no non-Brahmin will be invited to join the funeral nor will he think it necessary to join in the procession. If there is a festivity in the house of a Brahmin, no non-Brahmin will be called and no non-Brahmin will feel any wrong about it. Joys and sorrows of one caste are not the joys and sorrows of another. One caste has no concern with other castes. Even charity has become caste bound. Among Hindus there is no public charity in the sense of its benefit being open to all. You have Brahmin Charity for Brahmins. Within that you have Chitpavan Brahmin Charity for Chitpavan Brahmins only. Deshastha Brahmin Charity for Deshastha Brahmins only, Karhada Brahmin Charity for Karahda Brahmins only. You have Sarasvat Brahmin Charity. Within that you have Kudaldeshkar Brahmin Charity. One could go on with such instances *ad nauseum* to show the exclusive character of Hindu Charity—rather Charity among Hindus—for there is no such thing as Hindu Charity. Thus one Hindu will share nothing with another Hindu while they are alive. But they will be separate and exclusive even when they are dead. Some Hindus bury their dead. Some Hindus burn their dead. But those bury will not share the same cemetery. Each will appropriate a part of the cemetery to bury its dead. Those who burn will not burn at the same burning place. If they do, each will have a separate funeral pan.

Is there any wonder that the sentiment of fraternity is foreign to the Hindus? With a complete refusal to share the joys and sorrows of life how can the sentiment of fraternity take roots?

But the question of all questions is why do the Hindus refuse to share the joys and sorrows of life? It needs no saying that he refuses to share because his religion tells him not to share them. This conclusion need cause no surprise. For what does Hinduism teach? It teaches not to inter-dine, not to intermarry, not to associate. These don'ts constitute the essence of its teaching. All the shameful facts I have referred to, to illustrate the separate and exclusive character of the Hindus is the direct outcome of this philosophy of Hindusim. The philosophy of Hinduism is a direct denial of fraternity.

This brief analysis of the Philosophy of Hinduism from the point of view of justice reveals in a glaring manner how Hinduism is inimical to equality, antagonistic to liberty and opposed to fraternity.

Fraternity and liberty are really derivative notions. The basic and fundamental conceptions are equality and respect for human personality. Fraternity and liberty take their roots in these two fundamental conceptions. Digging further down it may be said that equality is the original notion and respect for human personality is a reflection of it. So that where equality is denied, everything else may be taken to be denied. In other words it was enough for me to have shown that there was no equality in Hinduism. But as Hinduism has not been examined so far in the manner I have done, I did not think it sufficient to leave it to implication that Hinduism was a denial of Fraternity and Liberty as well.

There is one final observation with which I wish to conclude this discussion with the profound observation of Lord Acton. The great Lord says that inequality has grown as a result of historical circumstances. It has never been adopted as a creed. It is obvious that in making this observation Lord Acton must have omitted to take note of Hinduism. For in Hinduism inequality is a religious doctrine adopted and conscientiously preached as a sacred dogma. It is an official creed and nobody is ashamed to profess it openly. Inequality for the Hindus is a divinely prescribed way of life as a religious doctrine and as a prescribed way of life, it has become incarnate in Hindu Society and is shaped and moulded by it in its thoughts and in its doings. Indeed inequality is the Soul of Hinduism.

Let me now turn to the examination of the philosophy of Hinduism from the point of view of Utility.

This examination of Hinduism from this aspect need not be long and detailed. For as Mill pointed out there is no necessary antagonism between justice and utility. In other words what is unjust to the individual cannot be useful to society. Apart from this we have before us the consequences of caste staring us in the face.

The ideal of caste was not mere ideal. The ideal was put into practice; was therefore something real. So that, in the matter of the Chaturvarna the Hindus have very faithfully followed the German Philosopher Nietszche who said "Realize the ideal and idealize the real."

The value of the ideal must be tested by its results. If experience therefore must be the criterion then the ideal of Chaturvarna stands thrice condemned. Purely as a form of social organization it stands condemned. As a producer's organization it stands discredited. As an ideal scheme of distribution it has miserably failed. If it is an ideal form of organization how is it that the Hinduism has been unable to form a common front. If it is an ideal form of production, how is it that its technique never advanced beyond that of the primitive man. If it is an ideal form of distribution, how is it that it has produced appalling inequality of wealth, immense wealth side by side extreme poverty.

But I do not wish to dismiss the subject so summarily, for I know many Hindus who claim great social utility to the institution of caste and praise Manu for having been so wise and so thoughtful not only in devising it but in giving it a divine sanction.

This view of the caste is due to taking the separate aspects of caste separately. One must take them in conjunction. The resultant social utility or disutility of caste can be ascertained only by putting together the separate aspects of caste and judge them in their combination. Following this line of attacking the problem, the following conclusions follow:—

(1) Caste divides Labourers (2) Caste disassociates work from interest (3) Caste disconnects intelligence from manual labour (4) Caste devitalises by denying to him the right to cultivate vital interest and (5) Caste prevents mobilization. Caste System is not merely division of labour. *IT IS ALSO A DIVISION OF LABOURERS.* Civilized society undoubtedly needs division of labour. But in no civilized society is division of labour accompanied by this unnatural division of labourers into wa-

tertight compartments. Caste System is not merely a division of labourers—which is quite different from division of labour—it is an hierarchy in which the divisions of labourers are graded one above the other. In no other country is the division of labour accompanied by this gradation of labourers. There is also a third point of criticism against this view of the Caste System. This division of labour is not spontaneous, it is not based on natural aptitudes. Social and individual efficiency requires us to develop the capacity of an individual to the point of competency to chose and to make his own career. This principle is violated in the Caste System in so far as it involves an attempt to appoint tasks to individuals in advance, selected not on the basis of trained original capacities, but on that of the social status of the parents. Looked at from another point of view this stratification of occupations which is the result of the Caste System is positively pernicious. Industry is never static. It undergoes rapid and abrupt changes. With such changes an individual must be free to change his occupations. Without such freedom to adjust himself to changing circumstances it would be impossible for him to gain his livelihood. Now the Caste System will not allow Hindus to take occupations where they are wanted if they do not belong to them by heredity. If a Hindu is seen to starve rather than take to new occupations not assigned to his Caste, the reason is to be found in the Caste System. By not permitting readjustment of occupations, caste becomes a direct cause of much of the unemployment we see in the country. As a form of division of labour the Caste System suffers from another serious defect. The division of labour brought about by the Caste System is not a division based on choice. Individual sentiment, individual preference has no place in it. It is based on the dogma of predestination. Considerations of social efficiency would compel us to recognize that the greatest evil in the industrial system is not so much poverty and the suffering that it involves, as the fact that so many persons have callings which make no appeal to those who are engaged in them. Such callings constantly provoke one to aversion, ill will and the desire to evade. There are many occupations in India which on account of the fact that they are regarded as degraded by the Hindus provoke those who are engaged in it to aversion. There is a constant desire to evade and escape from such occupations which arises solely because of the blighting effect which they produce upon those who follow them owing to the slight and stigma cast upon them by the Hindu religion.

The second mischief it dose is to dissociate intelligence from work and create contempt for labour. The theory of the Caste is that a Brahmin who is permitted to cultivate his intellect is not permitted to labour, indeed is taught to look down upon labour. While the Shudra who is required to labour is not permitted to cultivate his intelligence. The disastrous consequences of this have been well portrayed by Mr. R. C. Dutt.[24].....

Caste devitalizes a man. It is a process of sterilization. Education, wealth, labour are all necessary for every individual if he is to reach a free and full manhood. Mere education without wealth and labour is barren. Wealth without education and wealth is brutal. Each is necessary to every one. They are necessary for the growth of a man.

[24] *Quotation not given in the MS.*—Editors.

That the Brahmin should cultivate knowledge, Kshatriya should bear arms, the Vaishya should trade and that the Shudra should serve is presented as a theory of mutual interdependence found in the family. It is asked why should the Shudra need trouble to acquire wealth when the three Varnas are there to support him; Why need the Shudra bother to take to education when the Brahmin to whom he can go when the occasion for reading or writing arises; Why need the Shudra worry to arm himself because there is the Kshatriya to protect him? The theory of Chaturvarnya understood in this sense may be said to look upon the Shudra as the ward and the three Varnas as his guardians. Thus interpreted it is a simple and alluring theory. Assuming this to be the correct view of the underlying conception of Chaturvarnya it seems to me that the system is neither fool-proof nor knave-proof. What is to happen if the Brahmins, Vaishyas and Kshatriyas fail to pursue knowledge, to engage in economic enterprises and to be efficient soldiers which are their respective functions? Contrary-wise, suppose that they discharge their functions but flout their duty to the Shudra or to one another? What is to happen to the Shudra if the three classes refuse to support him on fair terms or combine to keep him down? Who is to safeguard the interests of the Shudra or for the matter of that of the Vaishya and Kshatriya when the person who is trying to take advantage of his ignorance is the Brahmin? Who is to defend the liberty of the Shudra or that of the Brahmin and the Vaishya, when the person who is robbing him of it is the Kshatriya? Inter-dependence of one class on another class is inevitable. Even dependence of one class upon another may sometimes become allowable. But why make one person depend upon another in the matter of his vital needs? Education every one must have. Means of defence every one must have. These are the paramount requirements of every man for his self-preservation. How can the fact that his neighbour is educated and armed, help a man who is uneducated and disarmed. The whole theory is absurd. These are the questions which the defenders of Chaturvarnya do not seem to be troubled about. But they are very pertinent questions. Assuming their conception of Chaturvarnya that the relationship between the different classes is that of ward and guardian is the real conception underlying Chaturvarnya, it must be admitted that it makes no provision to safeguard the interests of the ward from the misdeeds of the guardian. Whether the relationship of guardian and ward was the real underlying conception on which Chaturvarnya was based there is no doubt that in practice the relation was that of master and servant. The three classes, Brahmins, Kshatriyas and Vaishyas although not very happy in their mutual relationship managed to work by compromise. The Brahmin flattered the Kshatriya and both let the Vaishya live in order to be able to live upon him. But the three agreed to beat down the Shudra. He was not allowed to acquire wealth lest he should be independent of the three Varnas. He was prohibited from acquiring knowledge lest he should keep a steady vigil regarding his interests. He was prohibited from bearing arms lest he should have the means to rebel against their authority. That this is how the Shudras were treated by the Trayavarnikas is evidenced by the Laws of Manu. There is no code of laws more infamous regarding social rights than the Laws of Manu. Any instance from anywhere of social injustice must pale before it. Why have the mass of people tolerated the social evils to which they have been subjected? There have been social revolutions in other countries of the world. Why have there not been social revolutions in India is a question which has incessantly troubled me. There is only one answer which I can give and it is that the lower classes of Hindus have been completely disabled for direct action on account of this wretched system of Chaturvarnya. They could not bear arms and without arms they could not rebel. They were all ploughmen or rather condemned to be ploughmen and they were allowed to convert their ploughshares into swords. They had no bayonets and therefore everyone who chose ploughs did sit upon them. On account of the Chaturvarnya they could receive no education. They could not think out or know the way to their salvation. They were condemned to be lowly and not knowing the way of escape and not having the means of escape, they became reconciled to eternal servitude which they accepted as their inescapable fate. It is true that even in Europe the strong has not shrunk from the exploitation, nay the spoliation of the weak but in Europe, the strong have never contrived to make the weak helpless against exploitation so shamelessly as was the case in India among the Hindus. Social war has been raging between the strong and the weak far more violently in Europe than it has ever been in India. Yet the weak in Europe has had in him freedom of military service his physical weapon, in suffrage his political weapon and in education his moral weapon. Three weapons for emancipation were never withheld by the strong from the weak in Europe. All these weapons were however denied to the masses in India by Chaturvarnya. There cannot be a more degrading system of social organization than Chaturvarnya. It is the system, which deadens, paralyses and cripples the people from helpful activity. This is no exaggeration. History bears ample evidence. There is only one period in Indian history, which is a period of freedom, greatness and glory. That is the period of the Mourya Empire. At all other times the country suffered from defeat and darkness. But the Mourya period was a period when Chaturvarnya was completely annihilated, when the Shudras, who constituted the mass of the people came into their own and became the rulers of the country. The period of defeat and darkness is the period when Chaturvarnya flourished to the damnation of the greater part of the people of the country.

Caste prevents mobilization. Occasions arise when society must mobilize all its resources to one end in order to save itself from a catastrophe. To take a catastrophe like war, Society must mobilize all its resources for militarization. Every one must do war. Every one must be a soldier. Is this possible under the theory of caste? Obviously not. Indeed the destiny of a defeat which has been the lot of India throughout history is due to caste. Caste prevented general mobilization. Or the extent of mobilization was of a very limited character. Only the Kshatriyas were expected to fight. The rest the Brahmins and the Vaishyas were not armed and the Shudras who formed the large majority of the country were disarmed. The result was that once the small class of Kshatriyas were defeated by a foreign foe. the whole country fell at his feet. It could offer no resistance. It was not capable of resistance. Indian wars have been mostly wars of single battles or single campaigns. This was due to the fact that once the Kshatriyas fell everything fell. Why? Simply because there was no general mobilization and the theory deeply imbedded in the psychology of the people.

If these conclusions are sound, how can a philosophy which dissects society in fragments, which dissociates work from interest, which disconnects intelligence from labour, which expropriates the rights of man to interests vital to life and which prevented society from mobilizing resources for common action in the hour of danger, be said to satisfy the test of Social Utility.

V.

The Philosophy of Hinduism therefore neither satisfies the test of social utility nor does it satisfy the test of individual justice.

The result of my analysis is so odd that it will surprise many. Astonished some may even say that if the conclusions are so odd then there must be something wrong in my analysis of the philosophy of Hinduism. I must meet this objection. To those who refuse to accept my analysis I say that they find my analysis odd because they do not have a correct notion what is central in the philosophy of Hinduism. If they do they will feel no surprise at my conclusions.

This matter is so important that I must stop to explain it. It may be recalled that the foregoing analysis of the religious revolution showed that religious ideals as forms of divine governance for human Society fall into two classes, one in which Society is the centre and the other in which the Individual is the centre. The same analysis showed that for the former the appropriate test of what is good and what is right i.e. the test of the moral order is utility while for the latter the test is justice. Now the reason why the philosophy of Hinduism does not answer the test either of utility or of justice is because the religious ideal of Hinduism for divine governance of human society is an ideal, which falls into a separate class by itself. It is an ideal in which the individual is not the centre. The centre of the ideal is neither individual nor society. It is a class—the class of Supermen called Brahmins. Those who will bear the dominant and devastating fact in mind will understand why the philosophy of Hinduism is not founded on individual justice or social utility. The philosophy of Hinduism is founded on a totally different principle. To the question what is right and what is good the answer, which the philosophy of Hinduism gives, is remarkable. It holds that to be right and good the act must serve the interest of this class of supermen, namely, the Brahmins. Oscar Wilde said that to be intelligible is to be found out. Manu is neither afraid nor ashamed of being found out. Indeed Manu does not leave it to be found out. He expresses his view in resonant and majestic notes as who are the Supermen and anything which serves the interest of the Supermen is alone entitled to be called right and good. Let me quote Manu.

> X. 3. "On account of his pre-eminence, on account of the superiority of his origin, on account of his observance of (particular) restrictive rules, and on account of his particular sanctification the Brahman is the Lord of (all) Varnas."

He proceeds to amplify his reasons and does so in the following characteristic manner:—

> I. 93. "As the Brahmana sprang from (Prajapati's i.e. Gods)

mouth, as he was first-born, and as he possesses the Veda, he is by right the lord of this whole creation."

I. 94. "For the self existent (Svayambhu i.e.God), having performed austerities, produced him first from his own mouth, in order that offerings might be conveyed to the Gods and Manes and that this universe might be preserved."

I. 95. "What created being can surpass him, through whose mouth the gods continually consume the sacrificial viands and the manes the offerings to the dead?"

I. 96. "Of created beings the most excellent are said to be those which are animated; of the animated, those who subsist by intelligence; of the intelligent, mankind; and of the men, the Brahmanas".

Besides the reason given by Manu the Brahmin is first in rank because he was produced by God from his mouth, in order that the offerings might be conveyed to the Gods and manes. Manu gives another reason for the supremacy of the Brahmins. He says:—

I. 98. "The very birth of a Brahmana is an eternal incarnation of the sacred Law (Veda); for he is born to (fulfil) the sacred law, and becomes one with Brahman (God)."

I. 99. "A Brahamana, coming into existence, is born as the highest on earth, the lord of all created beings, for the protection of the treasury of the Law."

Manu concludes by saying that:—

I. 101. "The Brahman eats but his own food, wears but his own apparel, bestows but his own in alms; other mortals subsist through the benevolence of the Brahamana."

Because according to Manu:—

II. 100. "Whatever exists in the world is the property of the Brahmana; on account of the excellence of his origin the Brahmana is, indeed, entitled to it all."

Manu directs:—

VII. 36. "Let the King, after rising early in the morning, worship Brahmans who are well versed in the three-fold sacred science and learned (in polity), and follow their advice."

VII. 38. "Let him daily worship aged Brahmans who know the Veda and are pure. . . . ."

VII. 37. "Let the king, having risen at early dawn, respectfully attend to Brahman, learned in the three Vedas and in the science of ethics, and by their decision let him abide."

VII. 38. "Constantly must he show respect to Brahmans, who

have grown old, both in years and in piety, who know the scriptures, who in body and mind are pure; for he, who honours the aged, will perpetually be honoured even by cruel demons."

IX. 313. "Let him not, although in the greatest distress for money, provoke Brahmans to anger by taking their property; for they, once enraged, could immediately by sacrifices and imprecations destroy him with his troops, elephants, horses and cars."

Finally Manu says:—

XI. 35. "The Brahman is (hereby) declared (to be) the creator (of the world), the punisher, the teacher, (and hence) a benefactor (of all created beings); to him let no man say anything unpropitious; nor use any harsh words."

To conclude and complete the theory of supermen and of what is right and good let me reproduce the following two texts from Manu:—

X. 122. But let a Shudra serve Brahmans, either for the sake of heaven or with a view to both this life and the next, for he who is called the servant of a Brahman thereby gains all his ends.

X. 123. The service of the Brahmana alone is declared to be an excellent occupation for a Shudra; for whatever else besides this he may perform will bear no fruit.

And Manu adds:—

X. 129. No collection of wealth must be made by a Shudra, even though he be able to do it; for a Shudra who has acquired wealth gives pain to Brahman.

The above texts from Manu disclose the core and the heart of the philosophy of Hinduism. Hinduism is the gospel of the superman and it teaches that what is right for the superman is the only thing which is called morally right and morally good.

Is there any parallel to this philosophy? I hate to suggest it. But it is so obvious. The parallel to this philosophy of Hinduism is to be found in Nietzsche. The Hindus will be angry at this suggestion. It is quite natural. For the philosophy of Nietzsche stands in great odium. It never took roots, In his own words he was "sometimes deified as the philosopher of the aristocracy and squirearchy, sometimes hooted at, sometimes pitied and sometimes boycotted as an inhuman being." Nietzsche's philosophy had become identified with will to power, violence, denial of spiritual values, superman and the sacrifice, servility and debasement of the common man. His philosophy with these high spots had created a certain loathsomeness and horror in the minds of the people of his own generation. He was utterly neglected if not shunned and Nietzsche himself took comfort by placing himself among the "posthumous men." He foresaw for himself a remote public, centuries after his own time to appreciate him. Here too Nietzsche was destined to be disappointed. Instead of there being any appreciation of his philosophy, the lapse of time has only augmented the horror and loathing which people of his generation felt for Nietzsche. This is principally due to the revelation that the philosophy of Nietzsche is capable of producing Nazism. His friends have vehemently protested against such a construction.[25] But it is not difficult to see that his philosophy can be as easily applied to evolve a super state as to superman. This is what the Nazis have done. At any rate the Nazis trace their ancestry from Nietzsche and regard him as their spiritual parent. Hitler has himself photographed beside a bust of Nietzsche; he takes the manuscripts of the master under his own special guardianship; extracts are chosen from Nietzsche's writings and loudly proclaimed at the ceremonies of Nazism, as the New German Faith. Nor is the claim by the Nazis of spiritual ancestry with Nietzsche denied by his near relations. Nietzsche's own cousin Richard Ochler approvingly says that Nietzsche's thought is Hitler in action and that Nietzsche was the foremost pioneer of the Nazi accession to power. Nietzsche's own sister, few months before her death, thanks the Feurhar for the honour he graciously bestows on her brother declaring that she sees in him that incarnation of the "Superman" foretold by Zarathustra.

To identify Nietzsche, whose name and whose philosophy excites so much horror and so much loathing; with Manu is sure to cause astonishment and resentment in the mind of the Hindus. But of the fact itself there can be no doubt. Nietszche himself has openly declared that in his philosophy he is only following the scheme of Manu. In his *Anti Christ* this is what Nietzsche says:—

> "After all, the question is, to what end are falsehoods perpetrated? The fact that, in Christianity, `holy' ends are entirely absent, constitutes my objection to the means it employs. Its ends are only bad ends; the poisoning, the calumniation and the denial of life, the contempt of the body, the degradation and self pollution of man by virtue of the concept of sin,—consequently its means are bad as well. My feelings are quite the reverse, When I read the law book of Manu, an incomparably intellectual and superior work, it would be a sin against the spirit even to mention in the same breath with the Bible. You will guess immediately why; it has a genuine philosophy behind it, in it, not merely an evil-smelling Jewish distillation of Rabbinism and superstition—it gives something to chew even to the most fastidious psychologist. And, not to forget the most important point of all, it is fundamentally different from every kind of Bible: by means of it the noble classes, the philosophers and the warriors guard and guide the masses; it is replete with noble values, it is filled with a feeling of perfection, with saying yea to life, and triumphant sense of well-being in regard to itself and to life,—the Sun shines upon the whole book. All those things which Christianity smothers with its bottomless vulgarity; procreation, woman, marriage, are here treated with earnestness, with reverence, with love and confidence. How can one possibly place in the hands of children and women, a book that contains those vile words: "to avoid fornica-

[25] For this as also for facts which follow see M. P. Nicolas. "From Nietzsche Down to Hitler", 1938.

> tion, let every man have his own wife, and let every woman have her own husband. . . . . it is better to marry than to burn". And is it decent to be a Christian so long as the very origin of man is Christianised,—that is to say, befouled, by the idea of the immaculate conception?... I know of no book in which so many delicate and kindly things are said to woman, as in the Law Book of Manu; these old grey-beards and saints have a manner of being gallant to woman which, perhaps, cannot be surpassed. "The mouth of a woman", says Manu on one occasion, "the breast of a maiden, the prayer of a child, and the smoke of the sacrifice, are always pure". Elsewhere he says: "there is nothing purer than the light of the Sun, the shadow cast by a cow, air water, fire and the breath of a Maiden". And finally-perhaps this is also a holy lie:—"all the openings of the body above the navel are pure, all those below the navel are impure. Only in a maiden is the whole body pure."

This leaves no doubt that Zarathustra is a new name for Manu and that *Thus Spake Zarathustra* is a new edition of *Manu Smriti*.

If there is any difference between Manu and Nietzsche it lies in this. Nietzsche was genuinely interested in creating a new race of men which will be a race of supermen as compared with the existing race of men. Manu on the other hand was interested in maintaining the privileges of a class who had come to arrogate to itself the claim of being supermen. Nietzsche's supermen were supermen by reason of their worth. Manu's supermen were supermen by reason of their birth. Nietzsche was a genuine disinterested philosopher. Manu on the contrary was an hireling engaged to propound a philosophy which served the interests of a class born in a group and whose title to being supermen was not to be lost even if they lost their virtue. Compare the following texts from Manu.

> X. 81. "Yet a Brahman, unable to subsist by his duties just mentioned, may live by the duty of a soldier; for that is the next rank."
>
> X. 82. "If it be asked, how he must live, should he be unable to get a subsistence by either of those employment; the answer is, he may subsist as a mercantile man, applying himself into tillage and attendance on cattle."

Manu adds:

> IX. 317. "A Brahmana, be he ignorant or learned, is a great divinity, just as the fire, whether carried forth (for the performance of a burnt oblation) or not carried forth, is a great divinity."
>
> IX.323. "Thus, though the Brahmans employ themselves in all (sorts) of mean occupation, they must be honoured in every way (for each of) them is a very great deity."

Thus Manu's is a degraded and degenerate philosophy of superman as compared with that of Nietzsche and therefore far more odious and loathsome than the philosophy of Nietzsche.

This explains why the philosophy of Hinduism does not satisfy the test of justice or of utility. Hinduism is not interested in the common man. Hinduism is not interested in Society as a whole. The centre of its interest lies in a class and its philosophy is concerned in sustaining and supporting the rights of that class. That is why in the Philosophy of Hinduism the interests of the common man as well as of society are denied, suppressed and sacrificed to the interest of this class of Supermen.

IV. What is the value of such a religion to man?

Mr. Balfour in speaking on the merits of positivism as Religion asked the positivists certain questions which are worth recalling. He very pertinently asked;

> "What has (Positivism) to say to the more obscure multitude who are absorbed, and well nigh overwhelmed, in the constant struggle with daily needs and narrow cares; who have but little leisure or inclination to consider the precise role they are called on to play in the great drama of `humanity' and who might in any case be puzzled to discover its interest or its importance? Can it assure them that there is no human being so insignificant as not to be of infinite worth in the eyes of Him who created the Heavens, or so feeble but that his action may have consequence of infinite moment long after this material system shall have crumbled into nothingness? Does it offer consolation to those who are bereaved, strength to the weak, forgiveness to the sinful, rest to those who are weary and heavy laden?"

The same questions may be asked of Manu.

The answer to each one of them must be in the affirmative.

In short the philosophy of Hinduism is such that it cannot be called the Religion of humanity. That is why to use the language of Balfour, Hinduism, if it penetrates, does not vitrify the inmost life of ordinary humanity. Indeed if it does anything it paralyses it. There is in Hinduism no nourishment for ordinary human souls, no comfort for ordinary human sorrow, no help for ordinary human weakness. It leaves men in darkness face to face with the unthinking energies of nature, which gives them birth to which after a few fruitless struggles they succumb. Not less cruel than the crudest irreligious, does it leave men divorced from all communions with God.

Such is the philosophy of Hinduism. It is Superman's heaven and the common man's damnation.

I am conscious that my position regarding the philosophy of Hinduism will be assailed from different sides. So contrary it is to the current views about it that it is bound to be assailed. The attack may come from various sides.

It will be said that I am wrong in taking the Manu Smriti as the book of Hindu religion and that the true gospel of Hinduism is contained in the Vedas and the

Bhagwat Gita.

I am sure no orthodox Hindu will be bold enough to repudiate the authority of Manu Smriti as a book of Hindu Religion. Such a charge can be made only by some reformed sects of Hinduism such as the Arya Samajists. But there can be no doubt that this charge is not well founded. To refute this charge it is perhaps desirable to explain[26] how the Smritis obtained a place and position of authority among the Hindus.

The Smritis originally were a collection of rules relating to social traditions, customs and conventions approved of and recommended by those who were learned in the Vedas. For a long time these rules existed only in the memory of those learned in the Vedas, so they began to be called Smritis i.e. things which are remembered in contrast to Vedas or Shruti that is things which were heard. In the beginning the Smritis even when they were codified were treated as rules of inferior value as compared with the rules contained in the Vedas.

The difference in their authority and binding force was the result of the natural difference between the trustworthiness of what is heard as compared to what is only remembered. There was also another reason of this differentiation in the two sorts of Dharma Shastra literature. This was based upon the status of their authors. The authors of the Vedas were Rishis. The authors of the Smritis were only learned men. The Rishis were superior in status and sanctity than those who were merely learned. Consequently the Vedas were treated as more authoritative than the Smritis.

The consequence arising from this was well expressed in the Hindu theological formula according to which if there was a conflict in the rules of two Vedas on the same subject it meant option for a rule of Vedas cannot be deemed to be inoperative. On the other hand, in a conflict between a rule of Shriti and a rule of Smriti the rule of Shruti prevailed becuse for the reasons stated above Smriti was inferior in authority to the Shruti. But as pointed out by Prof. Altekar, the Smritis in course of time came to be invested with the same authority as belonged to the Vedas. Various means were adopted to accomplish this purpose. In the first place the authors of the Smritis were elevated to the status of Rishis. The early Dharma Shastra writers like Gautama, and Baudhayana were never given the status of a Rishi. But Manu and Yajnavalkya are reckoned as Rishis. By this means the status of the Smritis was equated to that of the Shrutis. The second means adopted was to regard the Smriti as the record from memory of a Shruti which was lost. Thus Smriti instead of being regarded as something quite different from Shruti came to be regarded as akin to and indistinguishable from Shruti. The result of these steps was a complete change in the rules regarding the authority of the two. Originally if there was a conflict between a Smriti and a Shruti, the Shruti prevailed. The new rule was that in case of conflict there was an option which meant that the Smriti rule was as operative as the Rule of Shruti. This new rule has been expressly laid down by Kumarila in his commentary on the Purvamimansa Sutra whereby the Smritis were made as authoritative as Shrutis.

[26] See the interesting article by Prof. Altekar—on "The Position of Smritis as a Source of Dharma" in the Kane Memorial Volume, pp. 18-25.

While originally Hindu Society was bound to the Vedas and could not follow any rule which was contrary to the Vedas, the new rule altered the situation and left it to the option of society either to follow the Shruti or the Smriti. But even this option was later on taken away. This was done by making the study of the Smritis as compulsory as that of the Shruti.

This was done gradually. In the first place it was suggested that the Shrutis and Smritis are the two eyes of the Brahamana, if he is devoid of one he becomes a one-eyed person. Then came the theory that Brahmanyam is possible only as the result of a joint study of both the Vedas and the Smritis. Finally came the rule according to which the study of the Smruti only was recognized and a contempt of the Smriti was made a sin and a person guilty of it was declared to be condemned to be born as a beast for 21 generations.

This is how the Smritis have been recognized as a source of Hindu Religion and there is no doubt that, to quote Prof. Altekar, the Smritis;

> "have played a great part in determining the features of many a social and socio-religious institutions and customs and in moulding the development of modern Hinduism."

It cannot therefore be maintained that I was wrong in taking Manu Smriti as containing the philosophy of Hinduism.

This work of elevating the Smritis to the status of the Vedas was undertaken by the Brahmins for a most selfish reason. The Smritis contain in all its wild and luxurious growth the doctrine of Caste, the doctrine of the superiority of the Brahmins, their rights and privileges, the doctrine of the subordination of the Kshatriyas and Vaishyas and the doctrine of the degradation of the Shudras. Such being the philosophy of the Smritis, the Brahmins were directly interested in investing the Smritis with the authority which was claimed for the Vedas and in which they ultimately succeeded to their advantage but to the ruination of the whole country. But conceding—which orthodox and pious Hindu would do—that the Smritis do not contain the philosophy of Hinduism but that the same is to be found in the Vedas and the Bhagwat Geeta the question is what difference would this make in the result.

It seems to me that it matters very little whether one takes the Smritis, or the Vedas or the Bhagwat Geeta.

Do the Vedas teach something, which is fundamentally different from what the Smritis do? Does the Bhagwat Geeta run contrary to the injunctions of the Smritis. A few illustrations will make the matter clear.

It is indisputable that the Vedas lay down the theory of Chaturvarna in what is known as the Purushasukta. This Purushasukta recognizes two basic principles. It recognizes the division of society into four sections as an ideal. It also recognizes that the ideal relationship between the four sections is inequality.

What the Bhagwat Geeta teaches is also beyond controversy. Its teaching may be summarized in the following four pronouncements made by Krishna in the Bhagwat Geeta.

(1) "I myself have created the arrangement known as Chaturvarna (i.e. the fourfold division of society into four castes Brahmins, Kshatriyas, Vaishyas and Shudras) assigning them different occupations in accordance with the native capacities. It is I who am the maker of this Chaturvarna."—Gita. IV. 13.

(2) "Even if it may be easier to follow the occupation of another *Varna* yet to follow the occupation of one's own Varna is more meritorious, although one may not be able to do it quite efficiently. There is bliss in following the occupation of one's own Varna, even if death were to result in performing it; but to follow the occupation of another *Varna* is risky."—Geeta. III. 35.

(3) "The educated should not unsettle the faith of the uneducated who have become attached to their occupation. He himself should perform the occupation of his Varna and make others perform theirs accordingly. An educated man may not become attached to his occupation. But the uneducated and dull-minded people who have become attached to their occupation should not be spoiled by the educated by putting them on a wrong path by abandoning their own occupation."—Geeta III. 26, 29.

(4) "Oh, Arjun! Whenever this religion of duties and occupations (i.e. this religion of Chaturvarna) declines, then I myself will come to birth to punish those who are responsible for its downfall and to restore it."—Geeta IV, 7-8.

Such is the position of Geeta. What difference is there between it and the Manu Smriti? Geeta is Manu in a nutshell. Those who run away from Manu Smriti and want to take refuge in Geeta either do not know Gita or are prepared to omit from their consideration that soul of Geeta which makes it akin to Manu Smriti.

Compare the teachings of the Veda, of the Bhagwat Geeta with what is contained in the Manu Smriti which I have taken as the text for elucidating the philosophy of Hinduism. What difference does one find? The only difference one can find is that the Vedas and the Bhagwat Geeta deal with General Theory while the Smritis are concerned in working out the particulars and details of that theory. But so far as the essence is concerned all of them—the Smritis, the Vedas and the Bhagwat Geeta—are woven on the same pattern, the same thread runs through them and are really parts of the same fabric.

The reason for this is obvious. The Brahmins who were the authors of the whole body of Hindu Religious Literature—except the Upanishad Literature—took good care to inject the doctrines formulated by them in the Smritis, into the Vedas and the Bhagwat Geeta. Nothing is to be gained in picking and choosing between them. The Philosophy of Hinduism will be the same whether one takes the Manu Smriti as its Gospel or whether one takes the Vedas and the Bhagwat Geeta as the gospel of Hinduism.

Secondly it will be contended that Manu Smriti is a Book of Laws and not a code of ethics and that what I have presented as a philosophy of Hinduism is only legal philosophy and is not the moral philosophy of Hinduism.

My answer to this contention is simple. I hold that in Hinduism there is no distinction between legal philosophy and moral philosophy. That is because in Hinduism there is no distinction between the Legal and the Moral, the Legal being also the Moral.

Not much evidence is necessary to support my contention. Take the meaning[27] of the word Dharma in the Rig Veda. The word Dharma occurs in the Rig Veda 58 times. It is used in six different senses. It is used to denote (1) Ancient custom, (2) Laws, (3) Any arrangement which maintains law and order in society, (4) The course of nature, (5) The quality of a substance and (6) Duty of good and evil. It will thus be seen that from the very beginning the word Dharma in Hinduism has a two fold connotation. It means both law and moral. That is one reason why in the philosophy of Hinduism there can be no distinction between legal philosophy and moral philosophy.

This is not to say that the Hindus have no code of morality. To be sure they have. But it is very pertinent to ask the nature and character of conduct, which the Hindu Code of Ethics declares to be moral.

To have an idea of the nature of conduct which the Hindu thinks moral, it is better to begin by recognizing that there are three levels of conduct,[28] which must be, distinguished. (1) Conduct arising from instincts and fundamental needs (2) Conduct regulated by standards of society and (3) Conduct regulated by individual conscience. Conduct on the first level, we do not call moral conduct. It is of course not immoral; it is merely unmoral. It is governed by forces not as moral in purpose but as valuable in result. The forces are biological or sociological or psychological. These have purpose, such as to satisfy hunger, or to forge a weapon against an enemy. But the end is one set up by our physical or instinctive nature. So long as this is merely accepted as an inevitable end and not compared with others, valued, and *chosen,* it is not properly moral. Conduct on the second level is no doubt social. Wherever groups of men are living there are certain ways of acting which are common to the group—"folkways." There are *approved* ways of acting, common to a group, and handed down from generation to generation. Such approved ways of acting are called the mores or the morals of the group. They imply the judgement of the group that they are to be followed. The welfare of the group is regarded as in some sense imbedded in them. It becomes the duty of the individual to follow them and if any one acts contrary to them he is made to feel the group's disapproval. We cannot strictly speaking call the conduct moral. Because the end is accepted as a standard of `good' prescribed by society. If it had spoken of a moral conduct it is only because it conforms to the mores or morals of the Society. It may be called customary morality. Conduct on the third level is conduct, which alone is truly and completely moral. That is because in it the individual *recognizes* the right or *chooses* the good, and freely devotes himself heartily

[27] What follows is taken from an article on the subject by Mr. Yeshwant Ramkrishna Date in a Marathi Magazine called "Swadhaya", Double No. 7-8. First year, pp. 18-21.

[28] In this I am entirely following the analysis given by Crawley and Tufts in their volume on Ethics.

to its fulfilment. He does not merely accept what is inevitable or follow what is approved by society. He values and chooses the end and becomes personally responsible. His is reflective morality.

V. On what level does Hindu morality stand?

Obviously it is not on the third level. This means that a Hindu is social but not moral in the strict sense of the term. A Hindu takes no responsibility for the ends he serves. He is a willing tool in the hands of his society, content to follow. He is not a free agent not afraid to differ. His notions of sin give remarkable proof of his unmoral character. Institutes of Vishnu gives a list of sins which are divided into nine classes:—

> 1. Deadly sins—*atipataka*. These are certain forms of incest, to be atoned for only by burning.
>
> 2. Great sins—*mahapataka*. These are killing a Brahman, drinking spirituous liquor, stealing the gold of a Brahman, connection with a Guru's wife; also social intercourse with those guilty of such sins.
>
> 3. Minor sins of a similar character—*anupataka*. These include the killing of certain other classes of persons, giving false evidence and killing a friend, stealing lands or deposits of a Brahman, certain forms of incest and adultery.
>
> 4. Minor sins—*upapataka*. Sins of false statement, neglect of certain religious duties, adultery, unlawful occupation, offences connected with marrying before an elder brother &c., not paying one's debts to the Gods, and manes, atheism &c.
>
> 5. Sins effecting loss of caste—*jatibramsakara*. Causing bodily pain to a Brahman, smelling things, which should not be smelt, dishonest dealing, and certain unnatural crimes.
>
> 6. Sins which degrade to a mixed caste—*samkarikarana*. Killing domestic or wild animals.
>
> 7. Sins which render one unworthy to receive alms—*apatrikarana*. Receiving presents and alms from despicable persons, trade, money lending, lying, and serving a Shudra.
>
> 8. Sins causing defilement—*malavaha*. Killing birds, amphibious animals, and aquatic animals, worms and insects; eating nutmegs or other plants similar in their effects to intoxicating liquors.
>
> 9. Miscellaneous sins—*prakirnaka*. Those not already mentioned.

This list of sins is not exhaustive but it, is long enough and illustrative enough to give us the idea which underlies the Hindu notion of Sin. In the first place it connotes the fall of man from a prescribed form of conduct. In the second place it means to be defiled, to become unclean. This is the root meaning of the term *Patak*.

It means *Patana* (falling away) and it means *Asowcha* (being rendered unclean). In either case sin according to Hindu notion is a decease of the soul. In the first sense it is merely breach of a rule of external conduct. In the other sense it is a defilement of the body to be cleaned and purified by both or by pilgrimage or by sacrificial offering. But it is never the spiritual defilement, which is associated with the harbouring of evil thoughts and purposes.

This shows the morality of the Hindu is purely social. This means that the level of his morality is purely traditional and customary. There are two evils of customary morality. In the first place there is no surety that it will always be charged with sincerity and purity of motive. For it is only when morality penetrates to the deepest springs of purpose and feeling in the individual that pretence will cease to find a place in human behaviour. In the second place customary morality is an anchor and a drag. It holds up the average man and holds back the man who forges ahead. Customary morality is only another name for moral stagnation. This is true of all cases where morality is only customary morality. But the customary morality of the Hindus has an evil feature, which is peculiar to it. Customary morality is a matter of meritorious conduct. Ordinarily this meritorious conduct is something, which is good from the general or public point of view. But among the Hinduism the meritorious conduct is not concerned with the worship of God or the general good of community. Meritorious conduct in Hinduism is concerned with the giving of presents, of good and of honour to the Brahmins. Hindu Ethics is worship of the superman.

What difference would it have made if I had taken Hindu Ethics as the basis for deducing the philosophy of Hinduism? Most students of Hinduism forget that just as in Hinduism there is no difference between law and Religion so there is no difference between law and ethics. Both are concerned with the same thing namely regulating the conduct of the low class Hindus to *subserve* the ends of high Caste Hindus.

Thirdly it will be objected that I presented an altogether false picture of Hinduism in as much as I have omitted to take into account the Upanishads which are the true source of Hindu philosophy.

I admit that I have not taken the Upanishads into account. But I have a reason and I believe very good reason for doing so. I am concerned with the philosophy of Hinduism as a part of the philosophy of Religion. I am not concerned with Hindu philosophy. If I were, it would have been necessary to examine the Upanishads. But I am quite willing to deal with it so as to leave no doubt that what I have shown to be the philosophy of Hinduism is the philosophy of Upanishads.

The philosophy of the Upanishads can be stated in very few words. It has been well summarised by Huxley[29] when he says that the Upanishad philosophy agreed:—

> "In supposing the existence of a permanent reality, or `substance', beneath the shifting series of phenomena, whether of matter or of mind. The substance of the cosmos was `Brahma', that of

[29] Evolution and Ethics, p. 63.

the individual man `Atman'; and the latter was separated from the former only, if I may so speak, by its phenomenal envelope, by the casing of sensations, thoughts and desires, pleasures and pains, which make up the illusive phantasmagoria of life. This the ignorant, take for reality; their `Atman' therefore remains eternally imprisoned in delusions, bound by the fetters of desire and scourged by the whip of misery."

VI. Of what use is this philosophy of the Upanishadas?

The philosophy of the Upanishadas meant withdrawal from the struggle for existence by resort to asceticism and a destruction of desire by self-mortification.

As a way of life it was condemned by Huxley[30] in scathing terms:—

> "No more thorough mortification of the flesh has ever been attempted than that achieved by the Indian ascetic anchorite; no later monarchism has so nearly succeeded in reducing the human mind to that condition of impassive quasi-somnambulism, which, but for its acknowledged holiness, might run the risk of being confounded with idiocy."

But the condemnation of the philosophy of the Upanishads is nothing as compared to the denunciation of the same by Lala Hardyal[31]:—

> "The Upanishads claim to expound `that, by knowing which everything is known.' This quest for 'the absolute' is the basis of all the spurious metaphysics of India. The treatises are full of absurd conceits, quaint fancies, and chaotic speculations. And we have not learned that they are worthless. We keep moving in the old rut; we edit and re-edit the old books instead of translating the classics of European social thought. What could Europe be if Frederic Harrison, Brieux, Bebel, Anatole France, Herve, Haekel, Giddings, and Marshall should employ their time in composing treatises on Duns, Scotus and Thomas Aquinas, and discussing the merits of the laws of the Pentateuch and the poetry of Beowulf? Indian pundits and graduates seem to suffer from a kind of mania for what is effete and antiquated. Thus an institution, established by progressive men, aims at leading our youths through Sanskrit grammar to the Vadasvia the Six Darshanas! What a false move in the quest for wisdom! It is as if a caravan should travel across the desert to the shores of the Dead Sea in search of fresh water! Young men of India, look not for wisdom in the musty parchments of your metaphysical treatises. There is nothing but an endless round of verbal jugglary there. Read Rousseau and Voltaire, Plato and Aristotle, Haeckel and Spencer, Marx and Tolstoi, Ruskin and Comte, and other European thinkers, if you wish to understand life and its problems."

[30] Evolution and Ethics, p. 64.
[31] Modern Review. July, 1912.

But denunciations apart, did the Upanishad philosophy have any influence on Hinduism as a social and political system? There is no doubt that it turned out to be most ineffective and inconsequential piece of speculation with no effect on the moral and social order of the Hindus.

It may not be out of place to inquire into the reasons for this unfortunate result. One reason is obvious. The philosophy of Upanishad remained incomplete and therefore did not yield the fruit, which it ought to have done. This will be quite clear if one asks what is the keynote of the Upanishads. In the words of Prof. Max Muller[32] the keynote of the Upanishads is `Know thy Self.' The `Know thy Self of the Upanishads, means, know thy true Self, that which underlies thine ego and find it and know it in the highest, the eternal self, the One without a Second, which underlies the whole world.'

That Atman and Brahman were one was the truth, the great truth which the Upanishads said they had discovered and they asked man to know this truth. Now the reasons why the philosophy of Upanishads, became ineffective are many. I will discuss them elsewhere. At this place I will mention only one. The philosophers of Upanishads did not realize that to know truth was not enough. One must learn to love truth. The difference between philosophy and religion may be put in two ways. Philosophy is concerned with knowing truth. Religion is concerned with the love of truth. Philosophy is static. Religion is dynamic. These differences are merely two aspects of one and the same thing. Philosophy is static because it is concerned only with knowing truth. Religion is dynamic because it is concerned with love of truth. As has been well said by Max Plowman[33]:—

> ". . . .Unless religion is dynamic and begets in us the emotion of love for something, then it is better to be without any thing that we can call religion; for religion is perception of truth and if our perception of truth is not accompanied by our love for it then it were better not seen at all; The Devil himself is one who has seen the truth only to hate it. Tennyson said "We must love the highest when we see it". It does not follow. Seen in pure objectivity the highest repels by its difference and distance; what we fear it, and what we fear we come to hate. . . . ."

This is the fate of all transcendental philosophies. They have no influence on the way of life. As Blake said "Religion is politics and politics is Brotherhood. Philosophy must become Religion that is it must become a Working Ethic. It must not remain mere metaphysics." As Mr. Plowman says—

> "If religion were a Metaphysic and nothing else, one thing is certain, it would never be the concern of the simple and humble men.
>
> "To keep it wholly in the realm of Metaphysic is to make nonsense of it. For belief in religion as in something not directly and vitally effective of politics is ultimately belief that is strictly speak-

[32] Hibbert lectures, 1878, p. 317.

[33] "The Nemesis of Ineffectual Religion"—Adelphi, January 1941.

> ing idiotic; because in the effective sense such a belief makes no difference, and in the world of time and space what 'makes no difference' does not exist."

It is for these very reasons that the philosophy of the Upanishads proved so ineffective.

It is therefore incontrovertible that notwithstanding the Hindu Code of Ethics, notwithstanding the philosophy of the Upanishads not a little not a jot did abate from the philosophy of Hinduism as propounded by Manu. They were ineffective and powerless to erase the infamy preached by Manu in the name of religion. Notwithstanding their existence one can still say

"Hinduism! Thy name is inequality!"

VI.

Inequality is the soul of Hinduism. The morality of Hinduism is only social. It is unmoral and inhuman to say the least. What is unmoral and inhuman easily becomes immoral, inhuman and infamous. This is what Hinduism has become. Those who doubt this or deny this proposition should examine the social composition of the Hindu Society and ponder over the condition of some of the elements in it. Take the following cases.

First as to the Primitive Tribes. In what state of civilization are they?

The history of human civilization includes the entire period of human progress from Savagery to Barbarism and from Barbarism to Civilization. The transition from one to other has been marked by some discovery or intention in some department of knowledge of Art resulting in advancing the onward march of man.

The development of articulate speech was the first thing which, from the point of view of human progress, divided man from the brute. It marks the first stage of savagery. The Middle period of the state of savagery began with the knowledge of the manufacture and use of fire. This wonderful discovery enabled man to extend his habit almost indefinitely. He could leave his forest home, go to different and colder climates, and increase his food supply by including flesh and fish. The next discovery was the Bow and Arrow. This was the greatest achievement of primitive man and marks the highest state of savage man. It was indeed a wonderful implement. The possessor of this device could bring down the fleetest animal and could defend himself against the most predatory.

The transition from Savagery to Barbarism was marked by the discovery of pottery. Hitherto man had no utensils that could withstand the action of fire. Without utensils man could not store nor could he cook. Undoubtedly pottery was a great civilizing influence.

The Middle State of Barbarism began when man learned to domesticate wild animals. Man learned that captive animals could be of service to him. Man now became a herdsman, no longer dependent for food upon the precarious chase of wild animals. Milk procurable at all seasons made a highly important addition to his dietary. With the aid of horse and camel he traversed wide areas hitherto impassable. The captive animals became aids to commerce, which resulted in the dissemination of commodities as well as of ideas.

The next discovery was of the Art of smelting iron. This marks the highest stage of advancement of barbaric man. With this discovery man became a "tool-making animal" who with his tool could fashion wood and stone and build houses and bridges.

This marks the close of the advancement made by barbaric man.

The dividing line which marks off Barbaric people from Civilized people, in the fullest sense of the word Civilization, is the art of making ideas tangible by means of graphic signs— which is called the art of writing. With this man conquered time as he had with the earlier inventions conquered space. He could now record his deeds and his thoughts. Henceforth, his knowledge, his poetical dreams, his moral aspirations might be recorded in such form as to be read not merely by his contemporaries but by successive generations of remote posterity. For man his history became safe and secure. This was the steepest assent and the climbing of it marks the beginnings of civilization.

Stopping here for the moment let us ask in what state of civilization are the Primitive Tribes.

The name Primitive Tribes[34] is expressive of the present state of people who are called by that name. They live in small-scattered huts in forests. They live on wild fruits, nuts and roots. Fishing and hunting are also resorted to for the purpose of securing food. Agriculture plays a very small part in their social economy. Food supplies being extremely precarious, they lead a life of semi-starvation from which there is no escape. As to clothes they economize them to a vanishing point. They move almost in a state of complete nakedness. There is a tribe, which is known as "Bonda Porajas" which, means "Naked Porajas." Of these people it is said that the women wear a very narrow strip which serves as a petticoat almost identical with what is worn by the Momjak Nagas in Assam, the ends hardly meeting at the top on the left thigh. These petticoats are woven at home out of the fibre of a forest tree. Girls wear a fillet of beads and of palmyra leaf and an enormous quantity of beads and neck ornaments extremely like those worn by many Komjak women. Otherwise the women wear nothing. The women shave their heads entirely. . . . . Of these Chenchus, a tribe residing near Farhabad in the Nizam's Dominions it is said that "their houses are conical, rather slight in structure made of bamboo sloping to the central point and covered with a thin layer of thatch..... They have very little, indeed, in the way of material effects, the scanty clothes they wear, consisting of a *langoti* and a cloth in the case of men, and a short bodice and a petticoat in the case of women, being practically all, besides a few cooking pots and a basket or two which perhaps sometimes contains grain. They keep cattle and goats and in this particular village do a little cultivation, elsewhere subsisting on honey and forest produce which they sell." Regarding the Morias, another Primitive tribe, it is stated the men generally wear a single cloth round the waist with a slap coming down in the front. They also have a necklace of beads and when they

[34] This and other information is taken from Census of India, 1931, Vol. I, part.

dance put on cock's plumes and peacock's feathers in their turbans. Many girls are profusely tattooed, especially on their faces, and some of them on their legs as well. The type of tattooing is said to be according to the taste of the individual and it is done with thorns and needles. In their hair many of them stick the feathers of jungle cocks and their heads are also adorned with combs of wood and tin and brass.

These Primitive Tribes have no hesitation about eating anything, even worms and insects, and, in fact, there is very little meat that they will not eat, whether the animal has died a natural death or has been killed four days or more before by a tiger.

The next group of the people he will come across are the Criminal Tribes.

The Criminal Tribes live not in Forests as the Primitive Tribes do but in the plains in close proximity to, and often in the midst of civilized life. Hollins in his "Criminal Tribes of the United Provinces" gives an account of their activities. They live entirely by crime. A few may be ostensibly engaged in agriculture, but this is only to cover up their real activities. Their nefarious practices find largest scope in dacoity or robbery by violence, but being a community organized for crime, nothing comes amiss to them. On deciding to commit a dacoity in any particular locality spies are sent out to select a suitable victim, study the general habits of the villagers, and the distance from any effective aid, and enumerate the number of men and firearms. The raid usually takes place at midnight. Acting on the information given by the spies, men are posted at various points in the village and by firing off their guns attract attention from the main gang which attacks the particular house or houses previously appointed. The gang usually consists of 30 to 40 men.

It is essential to emphasize the great part played by crime in the general life of these peoples. A boy is initiated into crime as soon as he is able to walk and talk. No doubt the motive is practical, to a great extent, in so far as it is always better to risk a child in petty theft, who, if he is caught, would probably be cuffed, while an adult would immediately be arrested. An important part is also played by women, who, although they do not participate in the actual raids, have many heavy responsibilities. Besides being clever in disposing off stolen property the women of the Criminal Tribes are experts in shop lifting.

At one time the Criminal Tribes included such well-organized Confederacies of Professional Criminals as the Pindharies and the Thugs.

The Pindharies were a predatory body of armed gangsters. Their organization was an open military organization of freebooters who could muster 20000 fine horse and even more. They were under the command of brigand chiefs. Chitu one of the most powerful commanders had under his single command 10000 horse, including 5000 good cavalry, besides infantry and guns. The Pindharies had no military projects for employing their loose bands of irregular soldiery, which developed into bodies of professional plunderers. The Pindharies aimed at no conquests. Their object was to secure booty and cash for themselves. General loot and rapine was their occupation.

They recognized no rulers. They were subjects of none. They rendered loyalty to none. They respected none, and plundered all, high and low, rich and poor, without fear or compunction.

The Thugs[35] were a well organized body of professional assassins, who, in gangs of from 10 to 100 wandered in various guises throughout India, worked themselves into the confidence of wayfarers of the wealthier class, and, when a favourable opportunity occurred, strangled them by throwing a handkerchief or noose round their necks, and then plundered and buried them. All this was done according to certain ancient and rigidly prescribed forms and after the performance of special religious rites, in which was the consecration of the package, and the sacrifice of sugar. They were staunch worshippers of Kali, the Hindu Goddess of destruction. Assassination for gain was with them a religious duty, and was considered a holy and honourable profession. They had, in fact, no idea of doing wrong, and their moral feelings did not come into play. The will of the Goddess, by whose command and in whose honour they followed there calling, was revealed to them through a very complicated system of omens. In obedience to these they often travelled even the distance of hundred miles in company with, or in the wake of, their intended victims before a safe opportunity had presented itself for executing their design; and when the deed was done, rites were performed in honour of that tutelary deity, and a goodly portion of the spoil was set apart for her. The Thugs had also a jargon of their own, as well as certain signs by which its members recognized each other in the remotest part of India. Even those who from age or infirmities could no longer take an active part in the operations used to aid the cause as watchmen, spies or dressers of food. It was owing to their thorough organization, the secrecy and security with which they went to work, but chiefly to the religious garb in which they shrouded their murders, that they could continue for centuries to practise their craft. The extraordinary fact was that Thugee was regarded as a regular profession by Indian Rulers of the day, both Hindu and Mahomedans. The Thugs paid taxes to the state and the state left them unmolested.

It was not until the British became rulers of the country that an attempt was made to suppress the Thugs. By 1835, 382 Thugs were hanged and 986 were transported or imprisoned for life. Even as late as 1879 the number of registered Thugs was 344 and the Thugee and the Dacoity department of the Government of India continued to exist until 1904 when its place was taken by the Central Criminal Intelligence Department. While it is not possible for the criminal tribes to live by organized bodies of criminals, crime continues to be their main occupation.

Besides these two classes there is a third class which comprises a body of people who are known as Untouchables.

Below the Untouchables there are others who are known as Unapproachables. Untouchables are those who cause pollution only if they touch. The Unapproachables are those who cause pollution if they come within a certain distance. It is said of the Nayadis—a people, who fall into the category of the Unapproachables, "that they are the lowest caste among the Hindus—the dog-eaters. They are the most persistent in their clamour for charity, and will follow at a respectful distance, for miles together any person walking, driving or boating. If any thing is given to

[35] Encyclopaedia Britannica, 11th Ed., Vol. XXVI, p. 896.

them, it must be laid down, and after the person offering it has proceeded a sufficient distance, the recipient comes timidly forward, and removes it." Of the same people Mr. Thurston says, "The subject (i.e. the Nayadis) whom I examined and measured at Shoranus, though living only about three miles off, had, by reason of the pollution which they traditionally carry with them to avoid walking over the long bridge which spans the river, and follow a circuitous route of many miles."

Below the Unapproachables are the Unseeables.

In the Tinnevelley District of the Madras Presidency there is a class of unseeables called Purada Vannans. Of them it is said, "that they are not allowed to come out during day time because their sight is enough to cause pollution. These unfortunate people are `compelled' to follow the nocturnal habits, leaving their dens after dark and scuttling home at the false dawn like the badger, the hyena, the avordvark."

Consider the total population of these classes. The Primitive Tribes form a total of 25 million souls. The Criminal Tribes number 4½ millions and the Untouchables number 50 millions. This makes a grand total of 79½ millions. Now ask how these people could have remained in the state of moral, material, social and spiritual degradation surrounded as they have been by Hinduism. Hindus say that their civilization is older than any civilization, that Hinduism as a religion is superior to any other religion. If this is so how is that Hinduism failed to elevate these people, bring them enlightenment and hope; how is it that it failed even to reclaim them; how is it that it stood with folded hands when millions and millions were taking to life to shame and crime? What is the answer to this? The only answer is that Hinduism is overwhelmed with the fear of pollution. It has not got the power to purify. It has not the impulse to serve and that is because by its very nature it is inhuman and unmoral. It is a misnomer to call it religion. Its philosophy is opposed to very thing for which religion stands.

Lector House believes that a society develops through a two-fold approach of continuous learning and adaptation, which is derived from the study of classic literary works spread across the historic timeline of literature records. Therefore, we aim at reviving, repairing and redeveloping all those inaccessible or damaged but historically as well as culturally important literature across subjects so that the future generations may have an opportunity to study and learn from past works to embark upon a journey of creating a better future.

This book is a result of an effort made by Lector House towards making a contribution to the preservation and repair of original ancient works which might hold historical significance to the approach of continuous learning across subjects.

HAPPY READING & LEARNING!

LECTOR HOUSE
LECTOR HOUSE LLP
E-MAIL: info@lectorhouse.com

9 789356 148024

9 789356 148024

Printed by Libri Plureos GmbH in Hamburg,
Germany